ERF B, C, CP & E-series at work

T0333213

Patrick W Dyer

Old Pond
PUBLISHING

ACKNOWLEDGEMENTS

My grateful thanks to the following for their help and support: Alan Watts, Clive Davis, Marcus Lester, Adrian Cypher, David Wakefield, Peter Davison, Steve Lynch, Paul Willis, John W Henderson, Rob Campbell, Iain Carr, Ken Beresford, Scott Whitehouse, Martin Aidney, Tony Jennings, my publisher and, of course, Linda and Jess Dyer.

ABOUT THE AUTHOR

Patrick Dyer, born in 1968, grew up during one of the most notable and exciting periods of development for heavy trucks and the last of the real glory days for trucking as an industry. This is reflected in his subject matter. Previously published in his growing 'Trucks at Work' series are: Scania's LB110, 111 and 141; DAF's 2800, 3300 and 3600; Ford's Transcontinental; Volvo's F88 and F89, followed by the F10 and F12; and Seddon Atkinson's 400, 401 and 4-11 and Scania 112 and 142.

DECLARATION

There were at least six recognised methods of measuring engine output for trucks during the period covered by this book. Manufacturers and magazines often quoted different outputs for the same engine using BS.Au, SAE, DIN and ISO systems, some gross and some net, much to everyone's confusion. Therefore, for clarity, only the figures quoted by ERF at the time are used throughout this work.

DEDICATION

This one is for Graham Baker, a good friend and self-confessed Gardner fan, without whose help and knowledge my Volvo F12 restoration would never have been finished. Thanks, Graham!

First published 2015

Copyright © Patrick W. Dyer 2015

Published by
5m Publishing Ltd,
Benchmark House,
8 Smithy Wood Drive,
Sheffield, S35 1QN, UK
Tel: +44 (0) 1234 81 81 80
www.5mpublishing.com

ISBN 978-1-910456-10-1

A catalogue record for this book
is available from the British Library

Front cover photograph

This superb early C-series was new to Gibbs in 1981. At the wheel is driver Eddie Thom, who completed over thirty years' driving with the company before retiring in the mid–1990s. *(Photo: ERF – courtesy of John W Henderson)*

Back cover photograph

Equally at home on the open road or multi-dropping in towns and cities, the flexible E10-325 was a great all-rounder. Manchester-based Norpak closed its business in 2007.

(Photo: Peter Davison)

Book layout by Liz Whatling
Printed by Bell & Bain

Contents

Foreword

By Reg Crawford

I write this foreword with a great deal of humility and more than a little trepidation — out of respect for ERF as a manufacturer that became a powerful symbol and representative of the 'Great British Truck Industry', and for Peter Foden CBE, its late Chairman, and his management team who I worked for and with during a brief period in the 1980s. My day job for many years now has been working as a business writer. I write and indeed 'ghost-write' editorial articles and other material on the subject of trucks, road transport and the people who work in the industry. It is a privileged position that has given me access, by necessity, to what is often proprietary information and people at all levels. That is why I have only been published under my own by-line on a few occasions and then mostly in 'in-house' articles and journals.

When Patrick Dyer approached me with a request to write this foreword, I was somewhat bemused as all my working life I have preferred to work in the background, believing that, as I am paid to write about the achievements of others, my customers and editors are, quite rightly, not interested in my opinions. At first, I was minded to turn down Patrick's request. However, on reflection, I decided to accept and present my personal observations for scrutiny in this excellent book.

The period covered in this book encompasses the launch of the B-Series in 1974 to the years immediately after the launch of the E Series in 1986. In that time ERF the company changed and grew in stature and its products developed into serious competition for the continental manufacturers who by then had successfully made huge inroads into the indigenous truck parc in all sectors from 16-tonners to multi-axle rigids and the big-hitter tractor units. Their success was down to building what customers needed as businessmen and women and what drivers wanted:

A consistent level of service, good back-up and a comfortable workplace for the driver — usually with a synchromesh gearbox. Until the advent of the E-series, ERF had tended to rely on the other, equally important operational virtues of good fuel economy, good payload and a long working life. In fact, ERF was known rather disparagingly by its German, Dutch and Swedish rivals as the no-nonsense builder of a 'gaffer's truck'. As Patrick Dyer points out in these pages, that meant a solid, dependable, 'no-frills' workhorse that delivered a good payload. But things were about to change.

In the mid-1980s, the company made a quantum leap, first with the CP and then with the E-series. ERF began to offer trucks that appealed to drivers and yet still delivered those qualities that had ensured the marque's appeal to hauliers and national fleets for so many years.

In my opinion, the success of the E-series was largely down to the foresight and relentless drive of the company's charismatic Sales & Marketing Director, Bryan Hunt. His enthusiasm for change and a positive turnround in the company's fortunes, both fiscal and in terms of its standing and repute as a manufacturer that could stand up to the might of the Europeans, carried his co-directors with him. Particularly so, Peter Foden, who was very much a champion of change and growth. In 1985 and '86, Bryan Hunt charged at any remaining naysayers in the wood-panelled offices of Sun Works and drove through changes in the product range that made it vastly more appealing to new customers as well as die-hard traditionalist hauliers, the bedrock of the customer base, who had unstintingly supported ERF through good times, bad and indeed very bad. I saw first hand how he would professionally and logically present the options to his colleagues. His background was as a consultant and a director at Cummins Engine Company and Solar Turbines. He was not an engineer but he knew how to persuade the engineering team and the board to accept that the product range needed to be rationalised. Gardner and Rolls-Royce engines continued to be offered, but were not in the 'preferred' spec. That rationalisation resulted in the CP range, followed by the E-series, and was patently good both for the business and its customers. Rationalisation of the driveline down to a simple and at the time highly controversial powertrain of Cummins, Eaton and Rockwell, meant that the manufacturing side of the business benefited from the cost reductions associated with reduced inventories and fewer parts in build lists reducing the number of 'snags' — faults found on inspection at the end of the build line. Customers could benefit from the reduced parts inventory if they ran their own workshops, and efficiencies were gained in training workshop technicians to service and repair a narrower range of components and assemblies. If a CP or E-series truck broke down, and if it was equipped with the rationalised driveline, the likelihood of the repairing dealer having the parts in stock increased exponentially. All in all, the CP and E-series represented an easier-to-understand and simpler, more modular concept that appealed to many operators who ran foreign-built trucks. It became a virtuous circle and ERF won many new customers as a result. So much so that, at a press briefing, cheekily held at Thame, the home of DAF Trucks in the UK in 1987, Peter Foden announced that ERF now had over 3,000 customers on its books.

The understated 'Built in Britain' badges on the cab tilt lock handles of the E-series were a tangible demonstration of ERF's core identity. It was a company and a brand that successfully offered its patriotism and 'Britishness' as one of its unique selling points. It appealed to customers, suppliers and employees alike. With the non-rusting sheet moulded compound plastic cab, its panels pressed by ERF Plastics at nearby Biddulph, and British Steel chassis frame rails, it was positioned as the epitome of the British underdog company battling it out with the dark forces of the continental manufacturers. The truck media were usually pretty friendly and forgiving of ERF and enjoyed playing along with the underdog theme when it suited.

During the development period of the CP and E-series, the company began to look at how truck cab styling could be used to modernise the model range and differentiate it from the competition. Since 1976, Peter Stevens, who later designed the exterior and interior of the McLaren F1 road car, was retained to provide design concepts and renderings for ERF. In 1986, he showed me his portfolio of beautifully drawn renderings of futuristic tractor unit concepts that he had presented to the board via ERF Chief Engineer Martin Harper. I can say, with some confidence, that if any of these concepts had been tamed and developed sufficiently so that they cost a competitive amount to build, and reached production, ERF would have gained a significantly greater share of the market and might, just might, still be building trucks today. But it would have been a bold move and one that ERF most likely could not have afforded financially to countenance. Lack of funding may have dogged ERF through the years, as did lack of real volume sales beyond its solid market performance; however, plucky under-dog or not, ERF the company and its many excellent people were never lacking in ambition or passion.

From tiny acorns

Although ERF came into existence following a difference of opinion amongst the board members of Foden regarding the way forward for road transport vehicles, it would be wrong to ignore the important engineering principles instilled and nurtured in the breakaway party, Edwin Richard Foden, during his time with the company founded by his father.

Foden was established in the mid-1850s as a manufacturer of agricultural equipment and took an early lead in the development of steam-powered traction engines towards the end of the 1800s. With a solid reputation for engineering excellence, and some forward thinking ideas for fuel-efficient boilers, Foden's steam traction engines evolved into steam wagons of note for the emerging road haulage industry in 1901.

Foden developed the steam wagon/lorry principle to its maximum potential over the next 30 years with final examples featuring pneumatic tyres, contemporary forward control cabs and near 60 mph capabilities.

However, despite his strong involvement in the design of these machines, Edwin was of the opinion that the type had had its day and that the future most definitely lay with oil-engine (diesel)-powered lorries. Like so many technological advances, the internal combustion engine, both petrol and diesel, had benefited from the rapid development that is often brought about by major conflict, in this instance WW1. These developments did not go unnoticed by Edwin, but most of the fellow board members at Foden did not share his opinion and continued to champion the steam wagon/lorry.

Frustrated, Edwin resigned at the age of 62, ostensibly to retire. However, his agenda was actually the forming of a new company with the sole purpose of producing the finest oil-engined lorries available.

E. R. Foden & Son, as the company was originally called, was established in 1933 with two other ex-Foden men, George Faulkner and Ernest Sherratt, and Edwin's son Dennis. The company set up an office in the conservatory of a house belonging to Edwin's eldest daughter, and with a plan to utilise proprietary components the team set about designing its first chassis. Suppliers such as Gardner, David Brown and Kirkstall were all keen to be involved and offered their products on a sale-or-return basis to help the company get off the ground. The design of a 4x2, 6-ton rigid with 15 ft body was completed very quickly and suitable premises to build the first example were offered in a recently vacated workshop belonging to J. H. Jennings & Sons at Sandbach. John Henry Jennings was a good friend of Edwin and production of the wood-framed aluminium-clad cab would fall to his coachwork company, thus marking the start of a mutually beneficial and enduring relationship for the two firms. The C14, as the lorry was called, was ready by the early autumn of 1933 and was given the chassis number 63, Edwin's age at the time. The design proved both capable and popular and a further 30 chassis were built by the end of the year.

Production grew rapidly over the next six years with 400-plus chassis per annum becoming normal by the time WW2 started in 1939. Despite the severe restrictions on raw materials caused by the activities of Hitler's U-boats, ERF was allowed to continue at virtually full production by the Ministry of War Transport, which also dictated where the finished vehicles would go. Naturally, the War Office became a big customer with a lightly militarised version of the then current C15 12-ton chassis being produced in large numbers for the Royal Army Service Corps, but civilian requirements were also met where possible to keep the home front functioning.

Despite its relatively small size, ERF weathered the postwar austerity years as well as any other heavy-vehicle manufacturer and managed to keep production at a reasonable level despite the continuing restrictions on raw materials. Developments were, however, kept to a minimum during this time, with little more than tweaks being applied to the C14 and C15 models that still formed the bulk of the range.

Prospects were raised with the lifting of steel rationing in 1953, sadly three years too late for Edwin, who died in 1950, and a palpable sense of optimism for the coming decade was in the air at Sandbach. Perhaps buoyed by this, ERF came up with some radical new designs, of which the most spectacular and important was probably the KV (Klear View) cab. This stunning curved design was beautifully smooth with large radius corners and featured an impressive two-piece wraparound windscreen that, with the omission of the traditional A-pillar, gave the driver a superb and unrestricted view. Gone, too, was the traditional exposed upright radiator, which was now hidden from view by the bodywork and a sleek oval grille that had seen brief service on a preceding model. The KV cab was designed and produced by Jennings, which used fibreglass for its construction, a first for ERF, as this material was well suited to form the rounded shape.

The KV cab was superseded by the LV in 1962. The new cab would serve ERF until the tail end of A-series production in 1975. During its 13-year production life, more than one manufacturer produced the LV for ERF and in a staggering number of versions. This 1969 example operated by Lowe was one of many such units that the company regularly despatched to the continent. Not even equipped with a basic sleeper conversion, drivers none the less slept in their cabs and their intrepid nature during this era of expanding continental routes always impresses the author.

(Photo: Colin Pearce)

The favourable costs of fibreglass production over tooling for steel or using aluminium over wood set the course for the majority of ERF cabs for the next twenty years. The KV got its debut at the Scottish Motor Show in 1953 and, with a winning combination of trusted mechanical components and groundbreaking style, was an immediate hit with operators and drivers.

1956 marked Peter Foden's return to the company, following two years of National Service. Peter, Dennis' much younger stepbrother and actually christened Edwin Peter, had first joined the company back in 1947 and, following the restructuring after his father's death, had become a director aged just 20. With his prior experience at ERF and two years' service with the Royal Electrical and Mechanical Engineers, Peter's position and contribution would be fundamental to the company's future direction and left him as the only logical successor for the position of managing director when Dennis died suddenly in 1960. Peter, aged just 39, was now about to oversee ERF as it truly got into its stride.

The 1960s were good times for the UK's truck manufacturers in general, but particularly ERF, where production soared, with nearly 1000 chassis produced in 1964 and well over twice that number in 1969. Peter's reorganisation of the company and his vision played a big part, but the company also displayed a knack of being ready with exactly the right product to meet major changes in legislation as they happened. Significantly, this was the case with the introduction of the 32-ton articulated limit in the middle of the decade.

Just as the KV cab had defined ERF trucks of the 1950s, its successor, the LV, would come to represent the 1960s. As with the KV cab before, Gerald Broadbent also designed the LV, but he had left Jennings by this time and now worked for Boalloy, which took on initial production, though later variants were also produced by Jennings.

Again of fibreglass construction, the cab marked another step forward for ERF and offered improved comfort for the driver in a high-datum, for the time, package. The cab was face-lifted over the years following its introduction in 1962, but received a significant update in 1970 for its role atop the chassis of the forthcoming A-series, which went into full production two years later.

The A-series was very important for the company and, as the immediate ancestor to the B-series, is particularly relevant to this book. With the exception of its fixed cab, the A-series marked the beginning of the modern era for ERF with a layout and components that were directly comparable to those of the last trucks produced some 30 years later.

By the early 1970s ERF was a much-changed company. Peter Foden's sweeping reforms and restructuring during the previous ten years had created a lean and hungry business with a thoroughly modern outlook. The A-series was, perhaps, the embodiment of the new ERF ethos, being highly rationalised to streamline production and make spares management much simpler. By this time, Cummins engines were becoming a more common fitment in ERF chassis, as was the case with this fine example driven by Arthur Barnshaw, which bears the engine manufacturer's logo on the grille. Note the elaborately shaped mirror arms. *(Photo: David Woodcock — courtesy of Paul Willis)*

By the time the LV cab was used on the A-series it had evolved into what was known as the 7LV. Whilst its ancestry was clearly recognisable, the latest update had done much to freshen up the design and, now free from old styling features such as the coach trim strips of its predecessor, it would remain looking fairly contemporary for the next few years. Gerald Broadbent, who also designed the KV back in the early 1950s, designed the LV cab; however, by this time he had moved from Jennings to Boalloy, which now took a share of cab production. Despite Boalloy's involvement with the LV cab, the company is far better known for its Tautliner trailers, a fine example of which we also see here. *(Photo: Steve Lynch)*

Known as the 5MW, ERF offered this Motor Panels steel cab as an option on some LV-equipped chassis in the early 1970s. Aimed mainly at the export markets of France, Belgium and Holland, the cab also found favour with a number of UK companies that frequented the continent, such as Beresford Transport and, oddly, Calor, which operated a lone example on its European traffic between 1973 and 1978 where it found favour with drivers for its comfort and the lusty performance of its 14-litre Cummins. There was also a 4MW version where the steps were removed and the wheelarch moved forward. This suited certain heavy haulage applications and was particularly popular in countries that ran a bridge formula for axle weights, such as Australia. Unfortunately, the cab did not tilt in either case, but it did provide the driver with spacious accommodation and a fully integrated sleeper. Note that the mirror arms retained a tailored shape, much like those of the LV.

(Photo: ERF — courtesy of Scott Whitehouse)

Following good sales of the 5MW cabbed truck in Northern Europe, ERF launched a revised version at the Brussels Show in 1973. The somewhat heavy-handed restyling exercise of the Motor Panels cab resulted in the brutal and imposing-looking 7MW. The truck was now officially known as the 'European' and crucially it had a tilt facility, making it the first ERF to be so equipped, just a whisker ahead of the B-series. That this steel-cabbed premium unit was developed and released, at no small cost, so close to the B-series, strongly suggests that ERF had no intention of marketing the new SP cab on the continent following its forthcoming launch and didn't expect UK operators to take them over the Channel either. This, and the fact that day cabs and digs were still very much a part of UK long-distance haulage, may also explain why ERF did not originally offer a sleeper cab version of the B-series. A 7MW European was among the six units to take part in Truck magazine's first ever Eurotest (1975), where it traded punches with, amongst others, the Scania LB140 and Volvo F89. The Cummins-powered ERF performed very well in this company, which shocked a few and surprised many. Like its predecessor, the European found its way into a number of UK fleets but sales were never large, although with a bigger international service network behind it the story might have been very different.

(Photo: ERF — courtesy of Scott Whitehouse)

The A-series, first shown in 1970, caused a major stir in the industry, such was its advanced nature. It was a competent truck with a high degree of parts compatibility throughout the range. It was well suited to current haulage requirements, particularly in the UK, and proved to be extremely popular, with high annual sales once production got into full swing in 1972. However, it did have one major failing. Whilst the cab itself was very good, offering the highest levels of comfort yet seen in an ERF, its fixed nature was a serious handicap by 1972, when any new premium truck had to feature a tilt cab if it was to compete with the strong continental designs that were flooding the market.

Luckily, by this time ERF was well advanced in the design of a new cab, which, along with further refined A-series components, would create the B-series of 1974.W

Known as the 'SP' cab, after its steel and plastic construction, the new assembly represented a break from tradition for ERF as it featured SMC (Sheet Moulded Compound) panels attached to a welded steel frame. ERF was already well versed in fibreglass production for its cabs, but the hand lay-up method was time consuming and the results inconsistent. Manufacture of panels in SMC involved the glass-reinforced resin and catalyst material being press formed at half a ton per square inch whilst heated at 140 degrees Celsius. This process allowed reliable mass production of cab panels with a fixed shape, size and thickness that could then be mounted to the steel cab frame via moulded-in threaded bosses. The panels had many advantages over steel, or other metals. For a start, tooling for SMC was far less expensive and the glass fibre material and process was far more forgiving on the dies, which therefore lasted much longer before needing replacement. The panels would, of course, be impervious to rust, but also most chemicals too and were unaffected by extremes of weather. Unlike a hand lay-up process, the finish was smooth on both sides and accepted paint very well. Panels of consistent shape and size could be produced very quickly. And whilst the cab's main strength came from the steel frame, the panels themselves were remarkably strong and resilient to minor impacts of the sort that would easily dent a regular steel panel.

Production of the SMC panels fell to ERF Plastics, which operated from a converted mill in Biddulph. This was formerly EB Plastics, a company that had been purchased by ERF Holdings to bring cab panel production in-house. One of the first jobs for this new venture was the production of cab components for the A-series.

The cab's steel frame, or skeleton, initially came from Motor Panels of Coventry. ERF already had an ongoing relationship with this British institution for the supply of steel cabs, mainly for its export models, so it was the perfect choice to produce the ERF-designed component. Comprising channel and box sections, the frame consisted of seven main parts. These were shipped to Sandbach, with a phosphate finish, where they would be built up in an entirely welded process before painting. ERF referred to the finished component as a cab sub-frame.

A completed SP cab was subjected to an impact test at the Motor Industry Research Association's (MIRA) Nuneaton facility in 1975. The test involved a 1.47-ton weight being swung into the front of the cab to represent a head-on collision. Damage, besides broken glass, was minimal with no incursion into the crew's space and only minor damage to the frame and panels. The results easily exceeded European requirements of the time. The steel frame, without SMC panels, was tested separately with similar results and also proved capable of withstanding a 17-ton static load in a roof crush test.

The interior represented another step forward for ERF. A very large glass area and cleverly angled side pillars created a light environment for the driver and gave superb all-round vision. Interior colours were a warm combination of tan and black, and Chapman suspension seats helped smooth any impact that might make it past the cab's suspension, which comprised coil spring dampers at the rear and rubber bushes at the front. Ahead of the driver was a neat and modern dash, with no exposed bulkheads or metal panelling. Through the two-spoke steering wheel was a clear view of the comprehensive instruments, which were dominated, first and foremost, by an EEC standard tachograph, with second billing given to the all-important rev counter. A bank of warning lights was positioned beneath the instruments in an angled panel, where illumination would be immediately obvious.

As the B-series was to be a rationalised range, the SP cab would have to serve across a wide range of weight categories. As such, there was a reasonably large interior tunnel to accommodate engines of 300-plus bhp. However, whilst denying easy cross-cab access, this feature was put to good use to house the parking brake, dual heater controls, document tray and ashtrays. In the centre of the dashboard just ahead of the tunnel was the vehicle's electrical centre containing the system's relays and circuit breakers.

Outside the cab was a clean and functional design, pleasant aesthetically and with a certain amount of presence courtesy of its wide black grille and quadruple headlight facade. The hydraulic cab tilt mechanism was operated by a pump mounted on the nearside of the chassis, just behind the front drop wing, which made easy work of tilting the cab to its maximum 68-degree angle for servicing and repair. Daily checks were performed via the grille, which opened on gas struts and a small flap at the base of the windscreen. The radiator header tank was located remotely on a gantry at the rear of the cab, from where it could be checked relatively easily from the top of the chassis.

The chassis itself was a model of simplicity featuring parallel frames of constant profile manufactured from high-grade carbon manganese steel. Side frame depths for tractors were 254 mm (10 inch) and 305 mm (12 inch) for rigids. However, as rationalisation was a key part of the range, the front section of the rigid chassis, which was otherwise different, tapered to the same 254 mm as that of the tractor units, so cross-members, engine mounts, etc. remained the same. In both cases the frame thickness was 8 mm. The chassis was assembled using a free-fit bolting method, which, featuring slightly oversized boltholes, allowed useful chassis flexing without damage and made maintenance and component replacement easier.

The suspension was virtually carried over from the A-series and, in the case of a tractor unit, involved long semi-elliptic springs and shock absorbers all around plus a shorter set of helper springs at the rear, which became active once the tractor unit was under load.

The triple circuit braking system featured four air tanks and was plumbed with a flexible reinforced nylon piping that was far more durable than traditional copper pipe and much easier to service and repair. The system featured an air dryer, rather than a wet tank, to remove moisture automatically. This prolonged the life of components and limited the possibility of icing in the system in extreme low temperatures.

Although heavily rationalised, the B-series still followed ERF's traditional policy of offering customers a wide choice of proprietary components. Engines were available from Gardner, Cummins and Rolls-Royce. Gearboxes came from either Fuller or David Brown and axles from Kirkstall or Eaton. The chassis, cab and the combination of engines, gearboxes and axles available gave the B-series a wide coverage of the weight categories between 16—37.4 tons.

 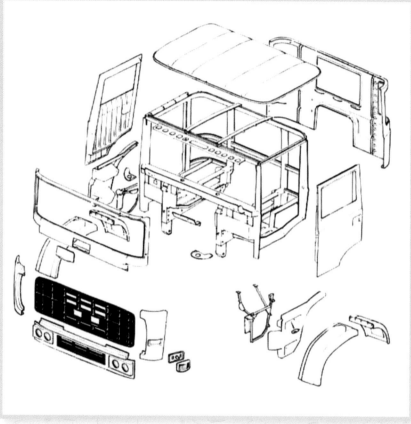

The heart of the SP cab concept was the robust steel frame originally manufactured as seven separate pieces by Motor Panels of Coventry for ERF to spot and seam weld into an assembly. The rigid structure was pre-drilled ready to accept the SMC panels, with integral mountings already moulded in, which would be attached during the build-up process that was quick and easy as a result. The parts drawing schematic shows the full cab sub-frame with the box sections for the seats, upper screen mounting and dashboard support panel in place too. The roof, whilst illustrated as one piece, comprised a left and right section. Similarly, the rear panel was made up of a centre and two corners and the windscreen a top and bottom and two sides, or A-pillars. This breakdown of parts and the unique bolt on construction made replacement of damaged panels easy for operators. Note the separate metal support for the cab step panel and the heavily ribbed door interior, the latter to give strength to this otherwise large flat area.

(Photo and illustration: ERF — Author's collection)

The SP cab was not only a revelation in its styling and construction on the outside, but the interior reached new standards of luxury for ERF too, with much more emphasis placed on driver comfort and environment than ever before. Sound insulation was particularly thorough, which, combined with the absence of engine access panels afforded by the tilt cab design, made this the quietest ERF yet. The A-series, which provided much of the B's underpinnings, was noted for its compliant ride, but the B-series also benefited from a coil spring and shock absorber cab suspension system, which was carefully matched to a top-of-the-range suspension seat from Chapman to eliminate all but the worst road shocks being transmitted to the driver. Ventilation and heating were not only first class, but also dual controlled to allow operation from the passenger seat. The large glass area made for a light workplace and the colours and quality of the interior fixtures and fittings made the cab a restful place.

The instrument panel, with its distinct raised centre section, was quite literally designed around the Lucas Kienzle EEC spec tachograph unit. Though not yet a UK requirement by law, this device, which we have since come to know so well, was a political hot potato at the time.

Note the tan finish of the engine cover on this prototype example, where early production trucks had a black finish. (Photo: ERF — Author's collection)

This 38G2 tractor unit, chassis number 28488, was registered in June 1975 and had the distinction of being the very first B-series tractor unit to enter service. Its Gardner 8LXB engine, nine-speed Fuller gearbox and Kirkstall rear axle made it the ideal truck for Beresford Transport, which had a long history of operating ERFs and a great deal of experience with this particular driveline combination. Not only was JRE 389N worked hard by the Tunstall-based firm, with day and night drivers keeping her rolling virtually 24 hours a day, but through great load planning and scheduling, she also ran loaded around 80 per cent of the time. Over a mixture of long night trunks and shorter multiple day trips, fuel returns from the Gardner were impressive, averaging 8.5 mpg. However, her early career was much easier and even had a touch of celebrity about it. JRE 389N was one of two tractor units and a rigid chassis that were used to launch the new B-series at the Earls Court Show in 1974. The other unit was powered by a Rolls-Royce Eagle whilst the rigid, an eight-wheeler, had a Cummins. The three Bs were joined on stand 87 by an example of the European with the 7MW steel cab and a couple of fire appliance chassis. Following the show, JRE 389N went on an extensive tour of ERF dealerships, which lasted several months, before Beresford's purchased her for £12,000. Beresford got a good deal on the price, but also the peace of mind that came from ERF's close monitoring of the truck through its early life. Frequent visits to nearby Sandbach resulted in numerous free modifications and improvements. (Photos: Ken Beresford)

Whilst this photograph appears to show a smart pair of early B-series 16-ton rigids, it does in fact show something quite different. A study of the chassis reveals the distinct upwards sweep of the earlier pre B-series four-wheeler, which would have featured the old LV cab. Examples of this type were still being registered on N-plates in 1975, as indeed were A-series tractor units. Of course, for a company like ERF, famous for its production-line flexibility, it would have been possible to engineer such a vehicle at a customer's request or even to use up otherwise redundant chassis. However, a closer look at the SP cabs also tells a story as they both feature the revised headlight panels introduced in 1978. So the author's conclusion is that these were originally LV-cabbed trucks, perhaps 64Gs that were fitted with SP cabs some time after October 1978. *(Photo: Steve Lynch)*

Despite the obvious excitement and interest surrounding the new tractor units, for initial B-series production ERF actually concentrated on the eight-wheeler chassis. This was due, in no small part, to the lack of an equivalent in the old A-series range in what was traditionally a very important sector for ERF and one to be ignored at its peril. One of the very first examples to enter service was an 8x4 tipper, HFL 440N, operated by Lincolnshire bulk haulier, Wherry and Sons. The vehicles spec was pure old-school ERF with a Gardner 6LXB engine, David Brown gearbox and Kirkstall rear axles. The truck pictured was another early 8x4 chassis, this time operated by Carnforth haulier G. E. Moore and, with the exception of a Cravens Homalloy body in place of the Wherry's Wilcox one, was to an identical spec. *(Photo: ERF — Author's collection)*

Two more examples of the 8x4 chassis, a hook or cable loader and bulk tipper, show the adaptability to purpose inherent in the ERF design. Just as the work to which this type of chassis was applied was tough, so too was the market and by 1975 a number of continental marques were making their presence felt with strong contenders in this field, not least DAF and MAN. However, also strong was Volvo, which marketed its Irvine-produced 8x4 F86 as a quasi-British product. Although heavily contested, this eased the conscience of some of the 1500 annual customers looking for 8x4 chassis in the UK, which made the Swedish machine a particular threat.

Richard Read operated a large number of B-series trucks in a variety of formats and was also an ERF distributor for the southwest.

(Photos: Adrian Cypher and Marcus Lester)

ERF introduced a six-wheel double drive chassis in 1975. Aimed mainly at the tipper market, it received its public debut in July at Tipcon, the Road Haulage Tipping Convention, in Harrogate. However, it was also well suited to a wide range of other duties in the 24-ton sector, not least petrol and oil distribution. Cummins and Rolls-Royce engines of 200 bhp plus were offered, as was the lower-powered Gardner 6LXB, which with the same 180 bhp as was offered in the eight-wheeler where it operated at its limit, still provided good performance at 24 tons if the David Brown six-speed gearbox was well manned. Depending on the bodywork and discharge method used, a decent payload in the region of 15—16 tons was possible. The ERF six-wheeler chassis was expensive in comparison to many of its competitors, and the class leader in sales terms was the Leyland Reiver, a rugged no-thrills workhorse. However, it must be remembered that many of the competitors were cheaper as they did not feature a tilt cab, and the field would not be level in that respect for a good few years to come. Note the later livery applied to MKK 35P. (Photos: Paul Willis)

Kent-based haulier Tomkinson ran a mix of early B-series, both artic and rigid, following good experience with the preceding A-series, and tended to favour the Gardner 8LXB with 240 bhp for its 32-ton operations.

The materials and construction of the SP cab were so radical that ERF thought it prudent to patent the design and process. As such, Swindell & Pearson of Derby submitted a Patent Application on behalf of ERF in September 1974. The application listed the inventors as Brian Townsend and Norman Reginald Cook. Whilst Cook was an engineer, Townsend handled ERF's publicity and was probably, therefore, involved with compiling and presenting the application.

The New Generation Mercedes range was also announced in 1974, but the German company's approach to cab design and manufacture could not have been more different. Mercedes went to great lengths to soften the visual impact of big trucks with this range and when comparing the two, it is hard to imagine that they complied with the same EEC regulations.

Note the air stack extension pipe on the rigid. This was introduced early in production to reduce in-cab noise levels. *(Photos: Steve Lynch)*

As its previous ranges had proved popular with oil companies big and small, ERF considered the articulated petrochemical sector of great importance. As such, it was vital that the B-series should hit the ground running in this respect. A full pet/reg or firescreen package was developed alongside the cab and made available from the start. Consisting of eight main pieces, plus brackets, the kit encapsulated the engine at the rear. Whilst most of it is hidden from view on this early example, the special panel behind the front wheel is clearly visible. This was a handed item available for either side and acted as an exhaust shield, but it was also used to form a useful step from which to access the chassis and had an anti-slip tread for this reason.

Also visible and part of the pet/reg package is the air intake elbow. *(Photo: Adrian Cypher)*

TESTING TIMES
B-series takes one on the chin

When the B-series was launched it was only available with a day cab and there are a number of reasons to suggest that ERF had no intention of offering a sleeper at all and was instead expecting its recently revised version of the European, with the steel 7MW cab, to fill that requirement. From an engineering point of view, the hardware assembly at the rear of the SP cab, which provided the cab support and mounting gantry for air tanks, air filters and header tank, was always going to be a problem if a sleeper version was going to evolve from the day cab. Also, though less critical, the standard chassis was too short to accommodate the extra cab length. To think that a company with the engineering prowess of ERF could have missed these facts in the design process is highly unlikely.

When the European failed to make a significant impact on the market but the B-series was an immediate hit, pressure from hauliers wanting sleeper versions of the SP cab, and lost sales to rivals already offering sleepers, might well have changed ERF's policy. Unfortunately, the result would now have to be reverse engineered, which, first and foremost, would start with a cab crash test performed at the MIRA test facility in August 1975. The test was crucial in establishing that the cab would meet the current vehicle test criteria of the Economic Commission for Europe (ECE) and so be to the standard of expected EEC regulations before ERF embarked on what was sure to be a costly engineering exercise.

The test was brutal and involved a 1.47-ton flat-faced steel plate being swung into the front of a chained-down B-series tractor unit in a pendulum motion from a height of over 20 feet. The massive impact resulted in only superficial damage and broken glass. Although the steel cab frame suffered minor damage, there was no incursion into the interior space.

Down but far from out, the B-series unit after the MIRA test with the minor cosmetic damage evident. Had this been the result of a real accident, not only would the crew have survived with only minor injuries, but the truck would have been easily returned to service thanks to the bolt-on SMC panel system.

(Photo: ERF — Author's collection)

The early to mid-1970s was a profitable time for the growing sector that offered after-market sleeper conversions to existing day cabs. Despite the influx of slick European sleepers and the steady demise of drivers' digs, British manufacturers were still dragging their heels on offering this logical development to long-distance trucks. At the time, companies like Locomotors of Andover were busy converting all manner of steel cabs at an average cost of £600 plus, good business indeed.

As an ERF dealer and operator, Richard Read was acutely aware of the demand for a sleeper version of the SP cab. However, the unique construction and materials used in the SP cab somewhat narrowed the field of companies that could undertake such a conversion, but through close collaboration with the coachbuilders Nash Morgan & Co., Richard Read was able to offer customers sleeper versions of the B-series from the end of 1975.

Eric Vick had no compunction about sending B-series units on gruelling trips to the Middle East, but for that harsh environment a full sleeper like this early conversion was essential. Note the blanked-out side window. *(Photos: Marcus Lester)*

Following ERF's takeover of the original company, to bring cab production in-house, J. H. Jennings & Sons Ltd was re-established in Crewe as Jennings Coachworks, from where it continued its rich history, which had started two hundred years previously. Despite their going separate ways, ERF continued a relationship with Jennings, and when the new Crewe company announced its sleeper conversion for the SP cab in April 1976 it was given full engineering approval from ERF. Indeed, it would be Jennings that ERF turned to for sleeper conversions until its own was available. The quality and durability of the product speaks for itself when viewing this fine example, which was 20 years old when photographed in 1995. Many a B-series has found a useful second or third life in the hands of steam preservationists. This one hailed from its birthplace and utilised its 180 bhp Gardner to great effect when moving its vintage road roller load.

(Photo: Martin Aidney)

ERF's official photograph for the new factory sleeper cab was released in September 1976 in the lead-up to the Motor Show at Earls Court and would feature in adverts and brochures. Although originally finished in the lurid orange of the B-series launch vehicles of two years ago, the truck would be painted in a bold Union Flag-derived livery for the show itself.

It may have had a prolonged gestation and caused a good many headaches to the design team during the process, but when it arrived the SP sleeper was a handsome beast. Not only good looking, the clever design with its high domed roof created an immense interior space for the driver and crew.

Note that this truck, as if to highlight its overseas potential to foreign customers, was produced in left-hand-drive format. *(ERF — Author's collection)*

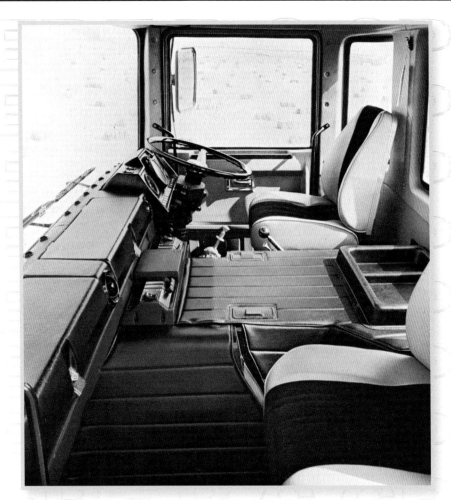

Some interior changes came with the introduction of the sleeper cab, chief amongst which was the new covering for the engine tunnel. This padded item served two purposes: firstly it acted as further sound insulation, answering some of the criticism of interior noise levels in the early cabs, and secondly it was a hard-wearing alternative to the strange painted finish adopted before, which easily became scratched in service and looked secondhand very quickly. No doubt, with the prospect of the crew crossing this area more regularly in the sleeper version, this was given some priority in the updates and the tailored item was probably not cheap to develop.

The raised roof, far from being a luxury appointment, was actually a necessity to provide the two berths with the required room under EEC regulations. This was a hangover from the fact that the air filters were still in the same position as on the day cab, which meant the first bunk could not be lowered. However, this happy accident of a feature gave the cab a very distinct look and also provided the occupants with much greater headroom whilst seated. (Photos: ERF — Author's collection)

Despite having sent its drivers abroad in day-cabbed trucks (see page 7), Lowe Transport did have their best interests at heart, and sleeper conversions, as seen here applied to the humble Atkinson Borderer, made a big difference. However, when the factory sleeper became available on the B-series, Lowe was quick to try it with a number of early units registered on R-plates joining the fleet. Here we see the company's first example alongside a group of the aforementioned Atkinsons in Antwerp docks and another parked up back home at the company's Paddock Wood depot.

(Photos: Colin Pearce and Steve Lynch)

The B-series represented an enormous leap forward when compared to other British trucks like the Atkinson seen here, which, although being replaced by the excellent Seddon Atkinson 400 range at this time, was still a current model when the B-series was launched. Although mostly hidden from view, the F88 was largely responsible for British manufacturers upping their game, such was its impact when introduced to the UK in 1967. The B-series had a great response from Great Britain, but ERF was too small to capitalise fully on the early interest it generated. One Evesham haulier who wanted to order 20 units in 1975 was told that he might get three by the end of the year! *(Photo: Steve Lynch)*

A tidy, if hard worked, B-series operated by Smith of Maddiston epitomises the workhorse nature of the range. Despite the technological leap and its modern appearance the B-series would always suffer the 'gaffer's motor' label to some extent. However, except maybe for the very lowest-powered examples, this was definitely unfair as the trucks generally possessed more than adequate performance for the task in hand and creature comfort was the equal of any European import at the time.

Note that the E and R are missing from the grille and the F centralised. The letters were fixed with a bolt from the rear and could not therefore be levered off from the front without damage. So unless this example had been left unattended in a particularly quiet location for some time, they were probably removed for a legitimate reason rather than pinched! *(Photo: Adrian Cypher)*

Despite the availability of Cummins and Rolls-Royce engines in the new range, and ERF's keenness to promote them, the Gardner option still remained popular, especially in traditional fleets like Jack Henley's, which had run large numbers of them in previous ERF trucks. Some viewed the Gardner engine, being normally aspirated, as out of step and old fashioned in the face of modern turbocharged units. However, its extreme reliability and remarkable frugality worked enormously in its favour.

Note the trademark Henley bumper bar and the home-fit auxiliary fuel tank. *(Photo: Steve Lynch)*

In 1975, during the frantic debates in the lead-up to the introduction of the EEC tachograph and the eight-hour driving day, there was even talk of imposing a maximum journey distance of 281 miles per day. As ridiculous as that was, it was also suggested that large rigids would be exempt from such a ruling. This might have been another factor that influenced early B-series rigid production taking precedence over tractor units and saw the potential return of the rigid eight as a dominant force in UK long-distance haulage. This fine example with Jennings sleeper conversion and long-range tank was almost certainly configured to take advantage of the maximum distance proposal, which, inevitably, never came to anything. *(Photo: Marcus Lester)*

In addition to the sleeper cab, ERF also debuted a new 6x4 bogie at the Earls Court Show in 1976. The new unit comprised Hendrickson suspension and Kirkstall axles and was shown fitted to a new chassis aimed primarily at the export market designated the 57C3. Broken down, that meant a 57,000 kg design weight, Cummins engine and three axles. The Cummins engine chosen for this application was the NTCE 350 producing 334 bhp and 930 lb/ft of torque, which drove through a Fuller 13-speed gearbox.

This impressive unit was one of a number built to a similar spec for Cunard Arabian Middle Eastern Lines (CAMEL). Based in Saudi, these trucks tipped loads that were delivered to the docks by Cunard ships, throughout the region. Cummins 375 engines and 16-speed gearboxes were fitted, as were the essential Kysor air-conditioning units. *(Photo ERF — courtesy of Scott Whitehouse)*

This rear three-quarter view, featuring another of Lowe's early factory sleepers, makes an interesting study and shows the depth of the new exterior panel that was installed just behind the door to cover the extension rearwards. Whilst the design retained the original rear corner and back panels, as used on the day cab, a new raised roof was required to give sufficient space inside for two bunks. The new roof, although backed up by a revised steel structure, was immensely strong in its own right, thanks to the SMC process and those deep grooves incorporated in its design. *(Photo: Paul Willis)*

As with the original SP cab, ERF returned to J. J Harvey of Manchester for the tooling to make the new sleeper panels, which were supplied under its Harvitool brand name. By this time Harvitool was an ERF operator, having taken delivery of a three-axle rigid chassis with double drive, similar to this example, which it used for nationwide delivery of tools, patterns and moulds to its customers. KBU 494P was a 25G3 powered by a 6LXB Gardner with a six-speed David Brown gearbox and featured dropside bodywork and a rear-mounted HIAB for autonomous loading/unloading. The truck was, no doubt, supplied at a good price as part of the deal for the tooling and completed 16 years service and over 750,000 miles before replacement, which came in the form of a 6x2 E8 in 1992. *(Photo: Steve Lynch)*

In the years leading up to the B-series' introduction, ERF had nurtured a healthy export market with its European cabbed trucks in the countries of Northern Europe and, slightly surprisingly given its operating restrictions and small annual market for trucks, Switzerland.

Mindful of the popularity of the wagon and drag combination in these countries, ERF offered a drawbar chassis from early on. Two Cummins-powered models were available, one with the NTE290 and one with the NTE350, whilst gearboxes were from Fuller and axles from Kirkstall. The drawbar chassis featured a tapered section just behind the gearbox, which allowed for a narrower chassis of 787 mm for its remaining length. With the extra room on the drawbar chassis, the larger 80-gallon diesel tank was made standard. (Photo: David Wakefield)

Eric Vick Transport was established in 1950 and had been running ERF trucks for a long time before the B-series was introduced. Gardner engines were highly regarded by the concern, particularly the eight-cylinder 240 which powered its top-weight tractors.

In 1975, Eric Vick signed up with fellow Gloucestershire haulier Richard Read of Longhope and Sandbach-based Jones Transport to form a separate company, Vijor International. The company was started by the trio to undertake an 84-load contract delivering sectionalised animal feed mills from the UK to the Middle East. A batch of P- and R-registered ERF Europeans undertook the gruelling 7000-mile journeys, often in convoy. Apart from air-conditioning units and fitted cookers and fridges, the trucks were standard units with Cummins power.

This gave Eric Vick a taste for the work, which continued with its regular fleet after the Vijor contract was fulfilled for the next decade or so. Much of the company's main work was European, with Holland, Belgium, France and Germany common destinations. However, the prestige of doing Middle East work was such that the destination became a proud part of the livery.

Note how poorly the A-series cab, this one with a sleeper conversion, compares to the new SP cabs of the B-series. Also, that the B-series units feature the new headlight mounts that were introduced around the summer of 1978. (Photos: Marcus Lester)

Trail Blazers was a marketing campaign launched in February 1978 and was perhaps indicative of ERF capitalising on the increased profits, up from £720,000 to £1,640,000, that the B-series had helped to generate so far whilst keeping the range, and its ongoing improvements, foremost in the minds of the truck-buying public.

A number of features were highlighted in the campaign, not least the quartz halogen headlights, which are seen here on this early demonstrator in the original-style mounts. This had changed by the time Truck magazine road tested another Trail Blazer demonstrator later in the year. By then, the twin Cibie units were mounted in a new one-piece panel that spanned the width of the truck. This gave the headlights better support, making them less vulnerable to vibration and the premature bulb failure of the original set-up. The new design also allowed the cab to be tilted over without the hassle of lowering them, as had been necessary before because of the extra depth of the box mountings. (Photo: ERF — courtesy of Scott Whitehouse)

The SP cab was granted a full UK patent in August 1978, nearly four years after the application was first filed, which protected the ERF design although the construction process remained pending, and would deter any jealous steel-bodied rivals from adopting the same techniques.

Whilst it was the SP's manageable tooling costs and ease of construction that benefited ERF, the biggest boon to the operator was the absence of rust in the cab panels, a malady that was still affecting some modern steel cabs at the time when only a few years old.

A comparison of these two examples reveals a detail difference in the apron panel below the main grille as the Bowkett unit is fitted with a front towing member. When specified, this optional item was bolted to the standard towing plates and the lower grille was deleted.

Note the door handle is missing on the Smith unit, as it is on the previous example from the same fleet on page 31. This item did, sadly, have a poor reliability record in the early years. *(Photos: Adrian Cypher)*

This pair would both have operated in the sort of environments where getting bogged down during the course of their duties was, at times, inevitable, and were thus fitted with the sturdy front towing member. Whilst functional for towing, this robust item also offered another line of defence for the front of the cab, protruding as it did past the bumper, not that it seems to have saved either vehicle here from damage to the latter item.

However, far more significant to operators of multi-wheelers was the new ERF non-reactive bogie, which went a long way towards stopping such vehicles getting bogged down in the first place. By balancing the reactive forces between the wheel sets of a bogie during braking, accelerating and cornering ERF's new system allowed the four driven wheels to be in contact with the surface more often than was possible with the traditional rocking beam set-up. The new system was marginally lighter than the ERF's standard one and worked via a system of bell-cranks and rods, which transferred the imparted loads. Additional benefits were better tyre and brake life and improved ride, particularly when on the highway, which, in back-to-back tests, allowed an increase of operating speeds of around 5 mph in most conditions.

Unveiled at the Scottish Show in November 1977, the new unit became available from January 1978. *(Photos: Steve Lynch)*

This stunning example, a 42C2 unit, was the hundredth B-series to enter service with Wincanton and was aptly named Centurion. It was fitted with the then new E290, an engine that offered the usual big Cummins performance, but with a useful improvement in fuel economy of 10— 15 per cent over its predecessor. With the space normally occupied by the diesel tank left vacant on this example, the extended wheelbase of 3.2 m, which was introduced for the sleeper-equipped chassis, is perhaps more obvious than usual.

Note the hydraulic tank for running discharge equipment and the rear fire-screening panel, the edge of which is just visible between the bottom of the cab and the top of the front wing. (Photo: ERF — courtesy of Scott Whitehouse)

Given the sound engineering, the quality engines and components, and the rust-free cabs that made up the B-series range, it is maybe unsurprising that so many would ultimately become yard shunters at the end of productive lives on the road. This example, which doesn't actually look beyond regular work, was part of the large Showerings fleet. Showerings had a number of premium drinks brands in its portfolio, including Babycham, but this livery was probably that of Gaymers Cider.

The truck looks to have been quite high spec when new, with Jennings sleeper, aluminium catwalk and professionally mounted spotlights in the bumper.

(Photo: Marcus Lester)

Onward Transport took a radically different approach with this shunter, which was based at the board mill in Purfleet during the 1990s. In this instance, the beauty of the SMC cab panels and steel frame construction was that it could easily be cut in this manner with an angle grinder or similar device. The author does not know quite what the rationale behind this modification was, but the Tugmaster dock spotter was, perhaps, an inspiration.

Onward had a large B-series artic fleet and tended to favour Rolls-Royce power units. (Photo: Clive Davis)

Despite the doom and gloom surrounding Great Britain's manufacturing sector at the time, there was still the odd success story in the late 1970s: in the truck sector, it was undoubtedly ERF, which, still independent, was enjoying year-on-year sales growth for the B-series. In ceramics it was H. & R. Johnson, then the largest producer of tiles in Europe and a world leader with its Cristal brand. And the family firm JCB had reached such a level of success and recognition with its products that the company name had become the generic term for any digger fitted with a backhoe attachment, which, with the notable exception of Hoover, was a feat achieved by few others before or since.

Fittingly, at the time, both H. & R. Johnson and JCB employed the services of Beresford Transport, a traditional English haulage company running traditional English trucks with traditional English power units (Gardner and Rolls-Royce), to distribute their respective products in Europe. Of the 60 or so B-series trucks operated by Beresford at the time, half were Gardner powered and half Rolls-Royce. Ken Beresford had no reservations in sending Gardner units to Europe, such was the company's experience with the 8LXB's legendary reliability, but his drivers preferred the extra power of the Rolls 265L, especially on hillier routes. (Photos: The Beresford Collection and Roy Palmer — courtesy of the Beresford Collection)

In February 1978, Cummins announced the Formula E 290 and to emphasise the premium role that ERF envisaged for the new engine in the B-series range, a 42C tractor unit with full factory sleeper would take centre stage at the NEC Show in October.

Despite the exciting engine developments, the biggest news at the NEC as far as the B-series was concerned was the heavily revised cab interior. A sweeping development, some elements of which had been introduced throughout the year on production trucks,

was topped by a stunning new blue-themed interior for the show vehicles. Originally called the SP MK 2, the development ultimately became known as simply the SP2. Driver/crew comfort was at the heart of the changes and a great deal of extra soundproofing was employed to that end, as was the change to a quarter light and separate side window in the doors, the latter specifically aimed at reducing wind noise. There was also a more user-friendly accelerator pedal and the steering wheel angle was changed to make it more

comfortable over long periods. Redesigned steps improved entry and exit, as did the new grab handles, which now featured a soft grip finish. Attention to detail created a usable table from the open glove-box lid and there was even a footrest in the passenger seat well in front of the relocated electrical centre.

Note that these interior shots illustrated a new padded steering wheel and brochures made mention of a redesigned item, but it was never adopted for the B-series. (Photos: ERF — Author's collection)

Whilst the day cab looked good, the sleeper version was stunning and the equal of any competitor in terms of design and execution. Big, roomy and now with pleasant soft-touch materials, it was the epitome of luxury. The engine tunnel in particular benefited enormously from the hardwearing Teracloth covering, which, though blue, somehow imparted a warmer feel to the interior. The dashboard, which was now constructed from a soft foam material, was totally redesigned and as well as being more ergonomic was now far more aesthetically pleasing with the look of a contemporary saloon car. Stowage

in general was improved and included a more useful oddments tray than the previous item, which was again located on the engine tunnel.

The overall effect, though spectacular, was far from traditional English and showed just how radical ERF had become in its approach to truck design. In fact, the look and feel was more than a little Gallic, which is curious as Renault was the next truck manufacturer to adopt a blue interior, for its Berliet cabbed R370 in 1983.

(Photos: ERF — Author's collection)

Alongside the top-spec Cummins-powered 42C, ERF showed a bread-and-butter day cabbed unit with the new Gardner 6LXC, which was aimed squarely at the up-to-32-ton sector as illustrated here by this Gardner powered unit. With just over the required output for this weight category, the 6LXC had been long awaited — having missed its intended debut at Earls Court in September 1976. The new version of the trusty 10.45-litre engine ran just 70 rpm faster than the 6LXB to produce 201 bhp, but Gardner were cagey, to say the least, about the exact nature of the other modifications that had gone into the unit. Designated by ERF as a 34G2, the unit on the show stand was a true lightweight in day cab form, coming in well under 6 tons, and was aimed at those wanting to shift loads of up to 21 tons or so frugally but without any thrills. (Photo: Steve Lynch)

Whilst the redesign of the dashboard was mostly to refresh the interior, improve its ergonomics and make it more attractive, it was also required to accommodate changes to the cab ventilation system and improve service access to items like the wiper motors and the clutch reservoir, all of which had received some criticism over the years. The original location for the clutch reservoir was behind the flap below the windscreen. Relocation to the main grille grouped it with other daily check items and allowed ERF to delete the flap, which resulted in a smoother frontal aspect.

This early SP2-cabbed example was converted with a mid-axle to allow 38-tonne operation post 1983. The slight angle of the wheel on the second axle suggests a degree of self, or positive, steering was available from this conversion. (Photo: Steve Lynch)

William Carman started Carman Transport after a spell in service following WW1. His first vehicle was an ex-War Department Leyland truck; however, Foden, and ERF following the split, became popular, particularly the latter, and Carman became very familiar with Gardner engines as a result. Much of the company's early work revolved around the Staffordshire potteries, bringing in raw materials and supplies whilst delivering out the finished products.

With the advent of continental services in the 1960s, Carman started Brit European Transport, and foreign trucks with better back-up abroad began to operate in the red and blue livery. However, by the mid-1970s Cummins-powered ERFs and Ford Transcontinentals were also regularly despatched to the continent and beyond.

CRF 936T was one of the first two E290-powered examples, plated at 38 tonnes, to enter service with Carmans. The company was delighted with the E290 fuel returns, which beat the best of the continental trucks on the fleet by 10 per cent.

When Carman first started going overseas and required trailers that could be custom sealed, it turned to the ex-Jennings man, and designer of the ERF KV cab, Gerald Broadbent at Boalloy to convert flats into TIR tilts. However, in both these cases purpose-built trailers are employed.

Note the doors on the front of the dry freight van: this was probably for carpet carrying, a particular contract for Carman. *(Photos: Steve Lynch)*

Peter Foden, whilst very much a patriot, was, first and foremost, a shrewd businessman with the best interests of ERF and its shareholders at heart. With this in mind, he had been championing the fitment of Cummins engines in ERF chassis as an alternative to Gardner and, to a lesser extent, Rolls-Royce since he took the reigns of the company in 1960. Whilst enjoying strong customer loyalty, the British engines just didn't have the international back-up enjoyed by Cummins, then the largest independent manufacturer of diesel engines in the world, which restricted the service options for ERF trucks abroad. Gardner units were fantastic, beautifully engineered creations and the only engines available with 40 per cent thermal efficiency, but the biggest, the 8LXB, was at its limit delivering 240 bhp, and by the mid-1970s that was no longer considered enough by the industry. Unfortunately, at the time, Gardner seemed adamant that turbocharging was not for them and with development of a new bigger engine economically unviable for the small Patricroft concern no increase in power looked likely. In addition to that, ever tightening emission legislation would be tough to meet without turbocharging. Rolls-Royce, on the other hand, had firmly embraced forced induction and was producing great engines with healthy outputs, particularly torque, but again, European coverage was not great.

With the E290, Peter Foden had the perfect engine with which to make his point to die-hard traditionalist customers. With power and economy in equal measure, the E290-equipped B-series became a remarkably strong contender for long-distance UK and continental haulage.

Compare the new-style Cummins badge, as affixed to the Harding unit, which accompanied the E290 launch with the earlier type above. *(Photos: David Wakefield and Marcus Lester)*

Re-cabbing a B-series was a great way to extend its life or change its operating possibilities by providing sleeper accommodation where before there was none, which is how we find this splendid early N-registered unit with an SP2 factory sleeper at the head of this line of Read trucks with after-market conversion. Reads, as an ERF distributor, would, of course, have had access to cabs from all sorts of sources, not least the factory, but ERF would also have been happy to sell a cab to anybody who required one. *(Photo: Marcus Lester)*

Unlike the Read truck, the SP2 cab and V-registration tally on this example operated by Shirley's. In fact, had it not been operated by such a high-profile firm and enjoyed such a long and distinguished career, the conversion may have gone virtually unnoticed. MRF 153V was actually first registered as NYB 66V and entered service with Wincanton's tanker fleet as a day-cabbed rigid eight with a Cummins 250 engine. Shirley's bought it with longer-distance operations in mind, so not only was it converted with the sleeper cab, but also, thinking the 250 a little low on power for its new role, an E290 Cummins.

Photographed in the late 1990s, the truck was getting on for 20 years old at the time.

Note the subtle airdam under the bumper and the slightly ironic fleet name, Metal Mickey. *(Photo: Clive Davis)*

This smartly presented unit was powered by a Cummins 250 and despite its remarkable condition was over two years old when photographed in mid-1982.

Cummins introduced the new, turbocharged 250, confusingly called the NT240, in 1979 to replace the old normally aspirated engine that had proved popular in the mid-power artics. Using many aspects of the E290, but not the famous 'big cam', the unit's main focus was on lowering emissions whilst still offering enough power for the sector. In this respect it scored well with around 235 bhp and 780 lb/ft of torque. Being based on the same 14-litre block as the more powerful engines in the range meant that durability was superb, too.

Note that this unit is fitted with corner wind deflectors as, despite its big radius corners and clean aerodynamics, the SP cab suffered from side-window fouling in bad weather. *(Photo. Martin Aidney)*

Although far more obvious on the right-hand unit due to the white finish, both these trucks have been fitted with a forward mud flap on the bottom of the front wheel arch. This in-house modification was presumably carried out to help reduce window fouling by directing dirty water further down before it had a chance to get into the air stream flowing off the front of the cab and, no duubt, it helped preserve the immaculate finish enjoyed by the Dickinson fleet.

Unswayed by the power and efficiency of the E290, Dickinson stuck to its favoured Gardner 240 for this pair.

Note the typo in the headboard of EJL 448V and the later C-series step ring on the far unit. *(Photo: Martin Aidney)*

In the face of the old guard, such as Wynns and Sunters, Leicester Heavy Haulage was very much the 'new kid on the block' when it was set up in 1972 by the entrepreneurial Brian Rodwell. Starting with one vehicle, quick expansion followed, through strong service values.

ERF figured largely from the start, mainly because of the great relationship that Brian enjoyed with the local dealership, Cossington Commercials. Cummins engines were preferred as they were the most powerful option and could be fitted with engine brakes.

Whilst far from heavy, these mobile crushers do, however, make an impressive load, especially in convoy with matching units. (Photo: Steve Lynch)

In the face of increasing acceptance of Cummins engines from other hauliers, Eric Vick remained resolutely behind the Gardner units of his 20-strong fleet, which spent its time travelling to and from the continent and beyond.

This unit, with full Middle East credentials, is seen returning through Dover, but the Gloucestershire firm also utilised a ferry service to Holland from Sheerness. Eric Vick considered it a good alternative, particularly for runs to Germany, as the driver could take a full rest period during the crossing, arriving refreshed and able to proceed immediately, having taken the requisite break whilst on board.
(Photo: David Wakefield)

George Machin founded his haulage company following the denationalisation of BRS, and by servicing the transport needs of the rich agriculture sector around Spalding enjoyed rapid growth. George started with a pair of secondhand Maudsleys and always favoured British trucks. In the 1960s the fleet virtually standardised on the AEC Mandator, which in turn led to Leyland Marathons. However, the varying quality and performance from the Leylands allowed ERF, Seddon Atkinson and Volvo in, the latter as the attributes of the F10 could not be ignored, in the late 1970s.

A pair of B-series units, registered on V-plates, were bought for evaluation. Powered by Cummins E290 engines they performed well on what was often intense, double-shifted work, which resulted in annual mileages of around 80,000 miles. (Photo: Steve Lynch)

Because of the huge cost involved in tooling for a truck cab, it was essential for all manufacturers to fully exploit its designs over a wide range of applications and weight sectors.

Whilst other manufacturers, such as Scania, DAF and Seddon Atkinson, offered trucks from 16 to 38 ton with the same basic cab, all but ERF had to reduce the width for the lightest applications, which inevitably meant many additional panels and tooling were required in the overall cab plan. For the M-series, ERF's 16-tonner, the lower grille panel was simply deleted to allow the cab to be lowered by 127 mm and the headlights mounted in a new bumper. To give cross-cab access, and the possibility of a third seat, ERF moved the engine back 300 mm and removed the engine tunnel. The result was a big, little 16-tonner. However, although sleeper versions were offered, the high roof was not. (Photo: Marcus Lester)

As with the M-series above, a sleeper conversion to this 6x2 rigid with 27-foot body has produced a truly versatile truck, which in this case was capable of 24-ton gross operation. Brian Harris, the operator of the M-series above, also ran a number of B-series trucks in this configuration, generally powered by a 6LXB Gardner, on UK general haulage.

ERF struggled to meet demand for sleeper cabs throughout B-series production and relied heavily on Jennings to pick up the slack. The conversion added around 550 mm to the length and utilised a completely new roof. (Photo: Steve Lynch)

The immediately recognisable livery of Knowles transport, applied, as ever, with great care and attention, makes this unit stand out as it passes through Dover.

Knowles had been B-series customers from the outset; Truck magazine actually borrowed an early P-registered unit from the company for its first ever B-series road test in 1975. That truck was Gardner powered, but Rolls-Royce engines were also popular in the Cambridgeshire fleet, powering both artic units like this and rigid bulkers.

Note the small RR badge on the lower grille of this Jennings-equipped example. *(Photo: Adrian Cypher)*

Operators with a preference for Rolls-Royce engines, but which required more power than the 265L, could satisfy their requirements with the 290L. Although it produced around 290 bhp and 876 lb/ft of torque, the 12-litre unit, much like the Cummins E290, was still working well within its maximum capabilities and at a lower maximum speed than its predecessor, which, if well matched with the driveline, gave good performance with economy and a long service life.

ERF dealer and haulage contractor S. Jones of Aldridge operated this unit in a customer livery, which was around five years old when photographed. *(Photo: Martin Aidney)*

Despite the continuous evolution of the B-series and even the SP2 restyling, the truck's big black grille remained a constant throughout production. Supported by twin gas-struts when open, the grille gave access to the oil dipstick and filler, power steering reservoir, windscreen washer bottle and, following the SP2 revisions, the clutch reservoir and cold start lever.

David Davies started his company in 1971 with one truck and grew it, through difficult economic times, to a peak of 22. Pre-merger Seddons and Atkinsons worked alongside Leylands and ERFs. Although this tidy unit was one of a batch with Rolls-Royce engines, Davies had favoured Gardner power for its great reliability since the start.

Note the useful, improvised step ahead of the diesel tank and the roof beacon, the latter fitted to most Davies units for abnormal load work. *(Photo: Steve Lynch)*

British Caledonian, or B-Cal as it was affectionately known to many, had, like all airlines, the need to move air-cargo pallets by road. A few years on from this B-series, Sutherlands handled the movements with a pair of DAF 3300s, but the author does not know whether that company was involved at this point. Whilst the day cab truck appears regular spec, possibly suggesting own account operation by B-Cal itself, the trailer was actually highly specialised. Five of these 40 ft GRP-bodied trailers with air suspension were delivered by S. Cartwright & Sons early in 1982. Specifically designed to handle air-cargo containers, they featured a tracking system in the floor with air-operated locking points.

The DC10 in the background was named Sir Walter Scott. *(Photo: Author's collection)*

Towards the end of 1980, ERF started to concentrate on weight-saving measures to broaden its appeal in a dire time of recession and cutbacks for the industry. To this end it showed three examples of its new lightweights at the NEC in October that year.

In tractor form, ERF claimed an extra half ton of payload was made possible by the changes, but the day cab unit with Rolls-Royce 265L was very much entry level.

This late example is near the end of B-series production and features at least one of the lightweight developments, the cylindrical aluminium diesel tank, which saved 50 lbs over the steel variant.

P & O had many different divisions, and Ferrymasters, which handled unit loads, made a massive £4.5 million investment in its trailer fleet in 1977. *(Photo: David Wakefield)*

THE C-series
Evolution not revolution

Like most of the B-series developments since 1974, the C-series was really just another evolution of improvements, but on this occasion ERF marked the changes with a new designation letter. The C36 was a direct development of the Super B lightweight and was officially launched as the first of the new C-series range in November 1981 at Kelvin Hall. The C36 incorporated a host of weight-saving features including taper-leaf springs, alloy diesel and air tanks and a new single air filter arrangement at the back of the cab. To create a really light 32-ton unit, ERF fitted the show truck with Gardner's new 6LXCT engine, a Spicer ten-speed gearbox and 10.5-ton Kirkstall axle. The turbocharged 6LXCT marked Gardner's first foray into forced induction and provided the little tractor with just under 230 bhp and around 670 lb/ft of torque. *(Photo: ERF — courtesy of Scott Whitehouse)*

C-designated tractors like these C40s started appearing following the show launch, but they were not really what was to become the full C-series spec. Indeed, when Truck magazine put a C40 around its Eurotest in the summer of 1982 it was still without some of the eventual C-series components. However, despite being an interim model, the Rolls-Royce 290-powered truck with Fuller nine-speed gearbox accredited itself very well, only beaten in journey times by a Renault R310, with 20 bhp more and another seven gears, and in fuel economy by a DAF 3300, which was slower around the course. Whilst not really chasing sales in Europe at the time, ERF entered the truck to show UK firms that did operate on the continent just what the C40 could do.

Both these examples are still fitted with the heavy steel tank from the old range, but the Owen Price unit, which must have been a little later, does have the correct C-series bumper.

Note the enormous air horns fitted to the Cooper truck.

(Photos: Martin Aidney and Adrian Cypher)

What ERF did establish from the start of the C-series was the substantial cab alterations, which resulted in a new designation of SP3. Changes on the inside were, once again, driven by major changes to the heating and ventilation system. In fact, ERF decided to design and patent its own heater for the SP3, which was then manufactured by Smiths. The subsequent changes to the dash can be seen here and it is worth noting that the duplicated heater controls for the passenger were dropped at this point, though the aperture, fitted with a blanking cover, remained for left-hand-drive versions. Although it is not shown in this early studio shot, there was also a shallow console in front of the dash centre section that provided a tray for oddments and a housing for a radio. There was also a change to the rear panel, which now featured a smaller window. This not only made things cosier for the top-bunk occupant, but also saved a little weight with the reduction of glass. The shallower window allowed for an additional storage bin below it on the rear wall. *(Photo: ERF — Author's collection)*

S. Jones, the main ERF dealership for the Midlands, held back on an order of 12 tractor units for its own haulage division until the full C-series spec was available. The trucks were required for its tanker fleet, which delivered hazardous loads to various destinations throughout Europe. As such, the fully fire-screened trucks were modified by the dealership in its own workshops to meet full ADR requirements. Having witnessed the power and economy of various demonstrators and test vehicles, some within its own fleet, the company opted for Cummins E290 power units.

AWD 636Y is seen posed for an ERF publicity shot with a 25,000-litre stainless steel tanker, whilst DWD 628Y is seen at Dover as it prepares to cross the Channel for another trip into Europe.

Note the redesigned towing member of the C-series that incorporated a central towing pin and the complex discharge equipment that cluttered the nearside of the chassis. (Photos: ERF courtesy of Scott Whitehouse and David Wakefield)

The biggest and most obvious difference between the SP2 and SP3 cabs on the outside was the entirely new front aspect, dominated by a handsome new slatted grille, which now comprised an upper and a lower panel. On the old design, the corner panels and grille were separate, but on the new cab the entire panel from the grab handles under the windscreen to the break line in the grille was one part. This not only allowed greater access when raised, but also streamlined parts and production for ERF. The grab handles were actually a very clever design incorporating the hinge mechanism for the panel, which was self-supporting when raised by twin gas dampers.

This well-looked-after example was at least seven years old when photographed delivering to Malmesbury Garden Centre.

Note the unofficial 'intercooler' badge on the bottom of the grille, suggesting that the truck was fitted with the Cummins E320. *(Photo: Clive Davis)*

Although the bolt-on SMC panels made damage repair a straightforward job for operators, there was still a desire by some to add extra protection to the front of their trucks. This practice, which for some reason was particularly prevalent with hauliers from Kent, stretched back to the days of the old LV cab and might just have been inspired by the double-bumper factory installation on Bedford's KM models.

Nicholls opted for this elaborate effort, as fitted to some ERF export models, for many of its C-series trucks, and given that the upper part of the cab was now one piece, the extra protection probably made economic sense. *(Photo: Steve Lynch)*

Calor bought its first B-series trucks in 1976 at a time when the company was enjoying an enormous surge in trade due to the popularity of the Super Ser cabinet heater, which utilised a 15-kg butane cylinder. An initial order for 4000 of these units from the Spanish manufacturer in 1970 had transformed Calor's business, and the need to move more and more cylinders around the country to feed demand meant large numbers of trucks. Whilst other makes came and went, often through company acquisitions, ERF were Calor's tractor of choice for the next 20 years. Cummins power units were definitely preferred, and by the time of the C-series had become standard, but some 8LXB and 6LXC Gardners were fitted to earlier examples.

As well as the burgeoning domestic cylinder market, Calor also undertook third-party work with its artic tanker fleet delivering throughout the UK and Europe, which is where trucks like this kept busy.

Up to 1990, Calor painted its chassis in this light grey finish with red wheels. Note the one-piece steel rear wings, which the company always fitted. *(Photo: Marcus Lester)*

Although it was founded in the same year as ERF, 1933, the Milk Marketing Board didn't operate any ERF trucks until nearly 40 years later, in 1972. By then, the company had been operating articulated units for four years, but its fleet of AEC Mandators was not proving up to the 24-hour, 365-day operation. An extensive trial of nearly every tractor unit on the market found the new A-series, with Cummins 220, well suited to the work and substantial orders followed. After its short production run, the baton passed to the B-series and, following its introduction, the C-series. By 1983, the MMB, now rebranded as Dairy Crest, was running 170 tractor units of which 150 were ERF, which made it one of ERF's most important customers.

Judging by its condition, this unit was brand new when photographed. *(Photo: Marcus Lester)*

To answer a long-running complaint regarding access to the SP and SP2 cab, ERF made a significant design change to that area for the SP3. As a result, the new step panel followed the ladder principle, in that the lower step protruded further out than the upper one, which made access, particularly when exiting, far safer. The lower step position was also higher than on the B-series, as it was found to be a more natural reach for the average driver, and its tread was wider without the restriction of the angled shape towards the rear of the old design that pushed the driver's foot rather too far forward, which was uncomfortable for some.

The new step detail is clear on this rather handsome example.

(Photo: John W Henderson)

The own-account operation of the Edinburgh Woollen Mill was highly specialised, being low weight, high cube and distribution based. Its challenging requirements were met by the use of drawbar combinations with demountable bodies. Based at the company's distribution depot in Langholm, the trucks operated over the length and breadth of the country and were mostly equipped with sleeper cabs. This fine example followed three similar-spec B-series units into service. The Bs were fitted with the Gardner 6LXC, so it is reasonable to assume that this unit, with Gardner Turbo badge, was running the 6LXCT.

A. C. Penman of Dumfries built the sturdy van bodies on Ray Smith demountable underpinnings. Keen to maximise on the economy of the Gardner engines, the trucks all featured this after-market roof-mounted wind deflector. *(Photo: Marcus Lester)*

ERF were well ahead of the game regarding the proposed UK weight increases under the Armitage report and showed its 6x2 twin-steer solution at the NEC in October 1982. Engineered for a 40-tonne GTW, as Transport Secretary Norman Fowler had put the tin hat on the 44-tonne proposal in the summer of 1981, the 40C unit would be ideal for the 38-tonne compromise expected by many.

The three-axle layout gave the show truck a GVW of just over 28 tonne whilst miraculously only weighing a shade under 7 tonne itself. Power was provided by a Rolls-Royce 290L, but Cummins and Gardner were listed as options. *(Photo: ERF — courtesy of Scott Whitehouse)*

Also celebrating 50 years in 1983, along with ERF and the Milk Marketing Board, was C. S. Ellis, and the fact was proudly marked on the front of its trucks. However, far from looking backwards, the company was embracing change early and following the introduction of the new 38-tonne limit put this handsome twin-steer unit into service. ERF commenced production of the twin-steer chassis in July 1983, making this an early example registered in the last two months of Y-registrations. *(Photo: Marcus Lester)*

ERF was keen to show that its C40 4x2 chassis was also suitable for 38-tonne when run as a two-plus-three combination. In fact, ERF had supplied a standard C40R2 tractor unit to Commercial Motor in 1982 to join a group test of, then, 32-ton tractors at the higher weight. At 285 bhp the Rolls 290L fitted to the test truck gave 7.6 bhp/ton, which seemed sufficient for the task, and the truck rode and handled very well. Being a day cab, it also scored well on payload managing 23 tons, despite the rather heavy three-axle tilt test trailer.
(Photo: ERF — courtesy of Scott Whitehouse)

The fleet of John Mitchell started to convert for 38-tonne operation almost as soon as the legislation went through. With a relatively new fleet of 4x2 units at the time, the preferred method for the Grangemouth concern was the addition of a Granning mid-life axle and Southworth Engineering converted around 20 units in this way. Around this time, the company was also busy converting a number of its skeletal trailers by adding extra twistlocks to accommodate 30 ft containers for a contract with International Ferry Freight. *(Photo: Adrian Cypher)*

Having shunned the principle for so many years, Gardner finally adopted turbocharging with the 6LXCT, which came on line in the summer of 1981. Forced induction gave the trusty 6-cylinder unit a healthy output of 230 bhp and a new lease of life in the up-to-30-ton sector. Following on from the success of that development, Gardner turned its attention to the 8LXC. This was the last update made to the 8LXB, the legendary 240/250 bhp engine that was held in very high regard by many in the industry, but which, sadly, had been left behind in the power race of the late 1970s when 290 bhp became the benchmark for 32-ton operation. In the face of a maximum weight increase in the early 1980s, the old engine was becoming largely redundant. However, adding a Holset 4LGK turbocharger brought the 8-cylinder unit up to 300 bhp, which made light work of 32-ton work and was more than adequate for 38-tonne operation. The 8LXCT had a remarkably flat torque curve that ensured 830 lb/ft of the maximum 868 was available from 1000 rpm right up to the maximum running speed of 1900 rpm. All of this was great news for those hauliers that had always sworn by the low running costs of a Gardner engine, and with the end to the practice of price loading Gardner-equipped chassis, it proved a popular choice in the C-series. (Photos: Steve Lynch and Marcus Lester)

Despite this new brown interior treatment for the C-series being shown at the October 1982 launch, it only started to filter through to production in the summer of 1983 and only appeared on the last of the Y-registered trucks.

The old blue interior had always divided opinion, but the new brown scheme seemed to meet universal acceptance from drivers and certainly provided a warm and restful environment. Apart from the colours, there were no changes to the design from the last revamp (see page 60) with the exception of a revised gear lever that now had the range change switch in the head of the unit, rather than the old plunger arrangement, which used to be attached to the lever below the knob.

Note how the seat pattern was repeated through the bunks.
(Photo: ERF — Author's collection)

Although this driver has the window at half-mast on this superb example from the McKelvie fleet, the ERF-designed heater/demister was a very effective unit that was more than capable of maintaining vision in inclement conditions such as here. Indeed, combined with the new brown interior, it made the SP3 cab a very comfortable place.

Also important in these conditions was the superb three-blade wiper system, driven by a single motor, which swept the large windscreen to good effect, and the twin two-jet washers. (Photo: Steve Lynch)

Part of the original design remit for the SP3 cab was the inclusion of headlight covers and a wash-wipe facility, neither of which ever made production; however, the rectangular headlight surround retained the lip for the abandoned covers and, although redundant in most cases, ERF did use it as a mounting point for protective mesh grilles on its heavyweight, Middle East-spec export models.

Note the much larger indicators that were also part of the SP3 package. *(Photo: Steve Lynch)*

Owner-driver Carl Jarman had been running an elderly Seddon Atkinson 400 before he traded up and bought this splendid C40 with Gardner 300 in April 1990. Despite being seven years old, the truck was in a very clean condition and the Gardner proved an economical and quiet engine. Unfortunately, the truck was stolen in April 1991 and Carl found himself back behind the wheel of another Seddon Atkinson, this time a 401.

Note the subtle airdam underneath the bumper. This was actually an E-series component, but one that was often retrofitted to C-series trucks by operators. *(Photo: Carl Jarman)*

Wincanton were happy to operate C-series trucks following the excellent, and ongoing, service from the numerous B-series trucks on the fleet. Operationally, day cabs were often preferable and, as here at 32 tons, the C36 chassis fitted the bill perfectly. Carmichael Fire and Bulk Ltd supplied many of Wincanton's bulk tankers around this time. Built on M & G running gear, the lofty design, at nearly 13 ft, was fitted with a Holmes 68 RBT blower powered by a 4-cylinder Ford diesel engine, which was mounted at the front of the tank in an acoustic cabinet. An interesting feature of the trailers was the collapsible handrail for the gantry that ran the length of the tank, which was air operated.

Despite the missing number from the registration, it is very possible that the well-worked shunter in the lower picture is FYA 166Y, and if not, it is definitely one from the same batch originally supplied to Wincantons. This plucky unit spent around 15 years as a shunter for Godwins and was only recently laid up at the time of writing in 2014. Note the later Wincanton livery. *(Photos: Marcus Lester & Clive Davis)*

The fleet name Tom Pearce had adorned the front of at least two previous trucks in the famous and much missed livery of Harris and Miners. Strictly speaking, the company had been just Brian Harris since 1978, when Brian took over the business following his father's death and bought out the Miners connection. This truck was among the very last to still feature both names.

As well as ratifying the business in 1978, Brian was also quick to change another aspect by universally adopting the sleeper cab across the fleet, something his father did not believe in, and all new tractor units from that point on were equipped as such.

At this time Jennings was still making up extra volume of sleeper cabs on an official basis for the factory with its flat roof conversion. (Photo: Marcus Lester)

Although an own-account operator with essentially one bulk product, Dairy Crest's operation was actually far from simple and its tractor choice had to be carefully considered. Its massive fleet of around 1,400 trucks was dominated by rigid tankers with the standard task of collecting milk from farms. The remaining 170 trucks (in 1983) were artic units, which hauled the bulk products in tankers and dry-goods trailers. The articulated tankers were split into two types, with the most important being the 'reload fleet', which collected the milk of two rigid trucks at a time from designated rendezvous points. Although the increase to 38 tonne was operationally useful to Dairy Crest, it could not adopt it across the board for many years as the update to equipment, particularly tanker trailers, was cost prohibitive. However, the dry-goods trailers could take advantage and a few tankers were converted for added capacity, so a pair of early twin-steers, with Cummins E290s, for three-plus-two running were purchased and an order for ten more placed. The impressive results of the E290 led to the engine being specced for all future 4x2 C-series trucks in the fleet too. (Photos: Marcus Lester and Steve Lynch)

The 1983 weight increase brought Britain into line with much of Europe and competitively closer to countries with still higher limits. Despite some recent hard times at home, continental business was booming, in particular with France, which enjoyed a near 50/50 export/import ratio with Great Britain. This made back-loads from our nearest European neighbour a near certainty and trucks bound for France could complete two trips a week, making it an attractive proposition for British firms.

Staffordshire hauliers Beresford and Carman already enjoyed good business in France and took full advantage of the increased limit with examples of the new twin-steer C40s, Beresford favouring Gardner power and Carman, Cummins.

Beresford had a big trailer fleet numbering 135 units at the time with its own dedicated trailer park to accommodate them, but this three-axle tilt was rare at the time when most were twin-axle tilts or flats from Crane Fruehauf, which made 6x2 units the sensible choice.

Both these companies represented UK haulage in the most professional manner with smart fleets of clean and well-maintained trucks driven by disciplined drivers.

Note that the Carman tanker is actually part of the company's French (Sarl) operation. (Photos: David Wakefield)

Depending on the engine fitted and the type of trailer being used, a 6x2 C40 could generally achieve a payload of around 25 tonnes, which made good economic sense to most operators. The extra axle on the tractor unit also meant a more compliant ride for the driver, which would have been especially welcome during the long Scotland to London trips undertaken by this example, and a stable platform for tricky, top-heavy, hanging loads such as beef carcasses. (Photo: John Henderson)

When designing the twin-steer chassis, ERF turned to Kirkstall, its oldest axle supplier, which provided its S62 tubular beam item to be fitted in conjunction with its D85 drive axle. The close-coupled axles were housed in a common bogie with low-maintenance rubber suspension with an airlift facility to raise the middle axle for short periods when extra traction was desirable.

Montgomery Transport, part of the massive Ballyvesey Holdings Group, was in its second decade when VIA 3488 joined the fleet as part of a batch of identical twin-steer C-series tractors. Ireland was not one of ERF's biggest markets so the factory capitalised on the order for publicity with two of the units, led by VIA 3588, featuring as the cover advert on the 7 January issue of Commercial Motor *in 1983.*

Note the non-standard diesel tank, which was fitted to all the Montgomery C40 twin-steer units. (Photo: Steve Lynch)

The rear window revision on the SP3 cab pleased many drivers as it offered more privacy without the loss of daylight and that 'over shoulder view', which could be useful on occasions. The reduced depth of the new item can be seen clearly in the photograph of the Nuttall truck. Considering the old window was the same depth as the side and corner glass, the reduction was considerable. Whilst not apparent from the interior, the modification was obvious from the outside as the depression for the bottom of the original aperture could still be seen.

For privacy and sleeping, the cab could be closed off by the eight individual curtains that ran in a track around the edge, but unlike some rivals, such as the Volvo F10/12, there was no transverse curtain and track, so the bunks could not be isolated for quick daytime rest breaks.

Note the small roof deflector on the Nuttall unit and the neat one-piece rear wings of the smart Gardner-powered Dawson truck. *(Photos: Steve Lynch and Marcus Lester)*

Calor, along with Shell and Lowfield Distribution, had been heavily involved in the design and consultancy process of ERF's twin-steer chassis, but whilst it was perfectly applicable to much of the company's work, there was still ample scope for capable 4x2 units in its fleet, like this one hauling a cylinder trailer, and they continued to be added after the weight increase.

Calor's opinion would have counted highly at Sandbach. Not only did it operate 350 trucks, the vast majority of which were ERF, but it also had a very accomplished engineering works at Rushden that undertook complicated conversion work on trucks and trailers. Another of its specialities was the construction of Calor's unique bull bar, which it manufactured from trailer gas pipe.

Note the angled air intake, which was part of the fire-screening package offered by ERF. *(Photo: Calor — courtesy of Iain Carr)*

ERF had long been the masters of chassis design, producing neat, uncluttered trucks that were correspondingly simple to service and maintain. With the C-series, and indeed the B before it, its designers reached such a level of perfection that an extra diesel tank or spare wheel carrier could be mounted without any of the disturbance or compromise to standard equipment that affected many a rival chassis. However, to the author's eye there was one small aesthetic downside to this, and that was the unfortunate gaping hole that would be left between the front and rear wheel on the nearside if the truck was not specced with any extras. *(Photo: Marcus Lester)*

Demo vehicles like this example of the S. Jones dealership division did much to convince operators looking for around 300 bhp that the E290 was a great engine with a superb balance of power and economy. The E290 had caused quite a stir when it was introduced in 1978 and changed many operators' perceptions about the big 14-litre Cummins, which was previously known for its wild drinking habits. However, that was nothing compared to the furore that surrounded the introduction of the LT10, Cummins' all-new 10-litre six. Originally mooted in 1974 and the result of a development programme that started in 1976, the new engine first appeared in manufacturers' chassis at the NEC in 1982. The engine was available in three power ratings of 180, 220 and 250 bhp with the highest intended for the up-to-38-tonne artic sector and 8x4 rigids, which made it ideal for the C36 tractor unit. The engine had undergone significant testing and trials by 1982, but the, almost, universal take-up by manufacturers was quite unprecedented considering it was a completely fresh design with no ancestry, other than the Cummins name, behind it.

Note the 'Cummins 10-litre 250' badge, which was slightly different from that of the launch vehicles at the show, where there was no reference to the output and the right-hand side was dominated by '10-litre' in larger writing. (Photos: Martin Aidney)

The job of the bulk tipper driver requires great skill where loading and distribution of the loose load is concerned. Only by experience will a driver learn the weight of different grains and the subtle weight changes brought on by moisture content. With a 4x2 unit the greatest worry would be drive-axle overload. Knowles Haulage did much to limit this problem with this fine-looking 6x2 twin-steer unit whilst also increasing its capacity for the 'paid by the kilo' loads.

Knowles would also have enjoyed reduced road tax on this three-plus-three combination and the extra axle on the truck would have given greater stability during the unloading process, which is always potentially dangerous. (Photo: Steve Lynch)

Beautifully presented, as were all Moffat trucks, this C-series also has that pleasing patina of use that marks out a true long-distance machine. Moffat was a big fan of the three-plus-two combination for 38-tonne operation. It was also keen on the C-series, with a blue interior 4x2 tractor, LSP 778X, fleet name Loch Garry, being added to the small fleet in the summer of 1982.

Much of Moffat's work involved hauling paper reels south from the nearby Tullis Russell mill, but it also ran fridges on international work and had previously handled tanker movement for Jet.

Moffat moved to Dalgety Bay, home of the trailer in this photograph, in the 1990s. (Photo: Peter Davison)

ERF actually considered its C57 chassis to be an option for three-plus-two 38-tonne operation, at least as far as advertising was concerned at the time. Of course, in reality the weight penalty of this 6x4 heavy would have ruled it out for most 38-tonne work, but as the chassis was available it was worth shouting about it. The design and layout of the C57 actually owed far more to ERF's export models than a standard UK truck. Saudi Arabia was a strong market for ERF and towards the end of 1981 it won a massive order from one customer, Taseco-TMS, which ultimately ran to 220 units by the end of delivery. The 57-tonne gross-weight tractors with Cummins E290 engines were based on the outgoing B-series at the time, but, apart from being day cabbed, were a similar spec to the superb C57 seen here. (Photo: Peter Davison)

Of course, apart from heavy haulage there was one other sector of UK haulage where a 6x4 back end did make economic sense and that was the 30-ton rigid. The rigid eight-wheeler had been the standard long-distance machine before the rise of the artic, but by the time of the C-series, and B before, the most common application for it would have been as an on/off road tipper/bulker or tanker. This example with Cummins engine was, therefore, rather unusual. Fitted with a neat curtainside body it was used by Healing's Flour Mill for deliveries to small bakeries. The truck is seen straddling a Zebra crossing on an early-morning delivery to a bakery in Marlborough. The truck eventually ended up operating with a Showman. *(Photo: Clive Davis)*

ERF's competent six-wheel chassis was perhaps more common on general haulage applications than the 8x4, striking a useful balance between vehicle size, performance and operating costs and payload, which could be 15—16 tons depending on spec. The market sector, in times of a healthy economy, could equate to 5000 chassis per year, but was hotly contested and very much layered. Despite the Gaffer's motor label, which still persisted in some areas, such as the more basic day-cab artics perhaps, ERF's six-wheeler was very much at the top end of a market that was dominated lower down by basic designs from Ford, Bedford, Leyland and Dodge. In this company the 6x4 C-series chassis was expensive, around £32,000 in 1983, but it came with a premium-class tilt cab and often engines that could equally serve in 30-ton rigids and 32-ton artics, which made them exceptionally durable and economic at the 24-ton limit for six-wheelers.

Although the payload of this example would have been eaten into by the extra weight of the sleeper conversion and the demountable refrigerated body, the operator must have considered the benefits of this high spec economic. *(Photo: Steve Lynch)*

The C-series trucks operated by C. & H. covered in the region of 50,000 miles per annum and were mostly powered by Gardner engines. Working alongside older B-series units, the trucks hauled paper and newsprint throughout the UK. Whilst its B-series trucks had mostly used the 240 Gardner, the later C-series trucks benefited from the extra power of Gardner 300 Turbo and, as most were bought following the weight limit increase to 38 tonne, were mainly 6x2 twin-steers like this. *(Photo: Steve Lynch)*

Although it may have had its troubles and was definitely behind the drag curve at the start of the 1980s, Gardner dramatically changed its game with the introduction of its turbocharged engines. The 8LXCT was particularly well timed and found a ready market for those, perhaps, more cautious hauliers that were about to move into the unknown with 38-tonne operation. Knowing that they could count on that legendary Gardner reliability and economy must have eased many a worry. In fact, the 300 bhp Gardner proved incredibly well suited to the task and was a popular choice. *(Photo: Steve Lynch)*

Two fine views of Lock's C-series unit, A546 LKL, firstly when newly commissioned and running at 32 tons and then later, with a few miles under her belt, at 38 tonnes with a tri-axle tanker. This unit was powered by an E290 Cummins and was entrusted from new to driver John Seabrooke. The truck was operated under contract to Gelpke & Bate, the chemical and solvent importer and distributor, and delivered loads such as paint thinners throughout the UK. Lock also ran trucks in Gelpke & Bate livery and operated the ERF alongside Scanias, MANs and even a number of White Road Commanders.

Note, in the later photograph, the missing covers for the spotlight apertures in the bumper and the steel diesel tank mounted on the nearside of the chassis that contrasts heavily with the beautiful polished aluminium one on the other side. This steel item does not appear to be of ERF origin and possibly started life on a Scania chassis. (Photos: Alan Lock — courtesy of Paul Willis)

The Australian company Pozzolanic set up operations in the UK in 1972 with a fly-ash treatment plant at Widnes. Fly-ash, the by-product of coal-fired power stations, can be converted, via a super-heating method, into extremely tough pellets with honeycomb centres that can be used as a very strong yet lightweight aggregate for the building industry. The company's first trucks in the UK were Mercedes LPS tractor units, which were painted in the livery of Aztec Bulk Lines, the company's dedicated haulage division. The company was very familiar with the Mercedes LPS from its home operations where it ran 150 examples. (Photo: Steve Lynch)

For the author, there is nothing quite as pleasing as a truck where the condition suggests a long, interesting and, hopefully, profitable career has taken place. This grand old lady was still working hard, with a deceptively heavy load, 20 years after being first registered. Sporting the over-spray evidence of a recent paint job, the unit was perhaps embarking on another change of ownership, perhaps with an owner-driver at the wheel.

Note the missing air horn trumpet on the nearside and the damaged name board, the aperture behind which contained a fluorescent tube and 24-volt inverter for illumination. (Photo: Peter Davison)

Presented, as usual, to the highest order, this Gardner 300-powered C40 of Brian Harris looks great coupled to this curtainsider trailer. Brian's policy of one driver to one truck did much to encourage the individual's pride in their machine and thus to look after it. Brian also had a policy that kept truck and trailer pairings together for most of their working lives; indeed, it was rare that a truck would ever uncouple its trailer except for routine greasing of the fifth wheel. Whilst the curtainsider looks great, Brian's trailer fleet was predominately made up of flats right up to the sad day of closure in 2001.

B379 UDV, fleet name Dartmoor Raider, was later fitted with the shallow E-series airdam under the bumper.
(Photo: Marcus Lester)

Leggett Freightways had a long history with Gardner power units that continued into the C-series era. Leggett's C-series tractors were mostly fitted with the 230 bhp 6LXCT, although if waiting lists had not been so long it would have opted for the all-new 12.7-litre 6LXDT, which produced 250 or 270 bhp. The company found Gardner power units very economic, returning 9 mpg at 32 ton, but more importantly durable and reliable, which suited its intense double shift operation, that also dictated the day-cab spec here, where mileages would run to 130,000 a year. *(Photo: Carl Jarman)*

Fine handling had always been a trait of the B-series 4x2 tractor unit chassis, a fact that allowed it to record excellent journey times, even against higher-powered machines, and the twin-steer layout, which had been in vogue before, was noted for its ride quality. So it was not surprising that the C-series twin-steer scored particularly well in this respect, filling the driver with such confidence that it could be safely hustled along at a good pace.

Spiers of Melksham will, perhaps, be best remembered for its long-serving fleet of secondhand AEC Mandators, the last of which was taken off the road when 14 years old in 1991, rather than any of its ERFs, but there is no denying how great that famous livery looked when applied to the big SP cab. *(Photo: Adrian Cypher)*

Suttons first incorporated the Union Flag in its livery to mark the Queen's visit to St Helens during her Silver Jubilee in 1977. The bold application across the grille and front panel of its fleet of around 80 trucks certainly made them stand out in traffic and emphasised the company's buy-British, where possible, policy. That policy saw the fleet consist almost entirely of ERF B- and C-series and Seddon Atkinson 400/401s. It was not by coincidence, either, that these two companies offered Gardner engines, Sutton's clear preference for power units.

Suttons landed a contract with the Bridgwater Paper Company in 1983 and over the next three years shifted 500,000 tons of paper with C-series and flat combinations like this. *(Photo: Steve Lynch)*

Unlike some rival twin-steer chassis, ERF's second axle was positively steered, which, combined with the excellent design and close attention to its geometry, not only ensured great handling and feel for the driver, but excellent and even tyre wear with no tendency to scrub the shoulders of the second axle tyres. In the normal course of things, the 10-ton Kirkstall drive axle took 62.5 per cent of the load imposed on the tractor unit, but the driver could temporarily override this if conditions deemed it necessary, as could have been the case here.

In addition to the factory-produced chassis, ERF also offered a service to convert customers' existing 4x2 units into twin-steers. (Photo: Steve Lynch)

Despite the fact that the C-series was the best truck range that ERF had ever produced, the company's share of the depressed market in the crucial 28-ton-plus sector was down to 7.3 per cent by 1984. Painful cost cutting and redundancies, which resulted in a workforce of less than half its strength of 1979, helped the company survive, but it was predicted that unless reversed this position would result in the closure of ERF by 1987. The answer was rationalisation. To a large extent this had started with the B-series range back in 1974, but, because of ERF's tradition of building to order it was still a long way from mirroring the streamlined production systems enjoyed by the strong European truck manufacturers. Management reduction and restructuring, with some key new appointments, brought fresh thinking and a new marketing approach, the result of which was to be ERF's saviour, the CP range.

This early press photo shows the truck without the subtle CP prefix that was later added to the Turbo badge on the grille. (Photo: ERF — courtesy of Scott Whitehouse)

The CP concept was based on the existing C-series range and actually was sold alongside it. There was no redesign of the cab exterior or the chassis, and apart from the single grille badge and the deletion of the door strip with model designation, it was indistinguishable from the C-series. However, the CP trucks featured a standardised drivetrain of Cummins engine, Fuller gearbox and Rockwell axles. This time-honoured combination was very well respected throughout the industry. Having come to be recognised in Europe during the 1970s, the Cummins/Fuller/Rockwell combination had been extremely popular in the USA for a long time prior to that. Consequently, it was proven over millions of long-distance highway miles.

Although Devon to Scotland is almost the maximum distance for UK operators, it would barely register for many US hauliers. In that respect, the CP driveline was, in effect, over spec, which resulted in great reliability and much higher mileages from the components. This suited Brian Harris' operation well and triggered a change from Gardner power.

This early CP was fitted with the Cummins 14-litre engine rated at 320 bhp and was photographed in Birmingham in 1990 (top), by which time it was the oldest truck in the Brian Harris fleet. *(Photos: Martin Aidney and John Henderson)*

Despite its big conversion policy over to three-axle units, operationally Mitchell's Transport still found there was a place for the classic 4x2 unit within the fleet. In this case it was probably the extra weight of the tipping skeletal trailer that dictated the use of such a unit rather than a heavier 6x2. The company landed the IFF contract to handle the rather unusual 30 ft containers following earlier experience of the type with Incobulk. Mitchell made significant investment for the contract, including a massive Caterpillar container handler, and was soon storing 900 containers at a time for IFF. (Photo: John Henderson)

W. J. Daniel put these six consecutively registered CP units on the road in August 1985. The patriotic West Midlands haulier used them to highlight his 'save jobs—buy British' campaign, the slogan for which was written on the front of his trailers. The CP range was all about saving British jobs, namely those at ERF and its suppliers, such as Cummins, which manufactured engines at its Shotts plant in the UK.

The E320 engine powered all of the six units, which also sported full air management as offered at the time.

Note the coach-type wheel trims fitted to the first two units. (Photo: ERF — courtesy of Scott Whitehouse)

The CP designation was generally thought to mean Common Parts or C-series to Preferred spec, but equally it could have been Cummins Preferred, especially from the point of view of the factory. Peter Foden was very keen on Cummins engines and had been trying to persuade his customers to buy them for years. It would have been entirely possible to streamline B- and C-series production with the 14-litre NTE range at its centre, much as Ford had done with the Transcontinental, but ERF had too many customers that were weight conscious and the 14-litre lump was too heavy for them. In this respect it was the introduction of Cummins' superb 10-litre engine that made the CP concept viable, especially as the engine manufacturer now offered an aftercooled version, the LTA, which produced 290 bhp. With Cummins providing the engines for the CP range, ERF could span the 250—350 bhp sectors with the two basic engines with various outputs, and everything below 320 bhp would come via the lightweight LT and LTA10.

The 10-litre-powered CP tractors were identifiable by the airstack location on the nearside of the cab. This pair operated by Carman Transport look factory fresh in the top picture, whilst the second unit has a few miles under its wheels in the lower one. (Photos: David Wakefield & Steve Lynch)

The CP-series was comprehensive with 11 chassis of 4x2, 6x2 and 6x4 configuration covering the 28—38-tonne sectors, but it did not extend to rigids. As with the standard C-series tractors, customers could still spec a six-wheeler rigid chassis as they pleased. This example has a heavy-duty 6x4 bogie and although it probably operated solo, would have made a handsome drawbar combination.

Note the angled air intake behind the cab. This was usually part of the firescreen package and was probably fitted here as it offered greater clearance between the cab and the headboard. Alternatively, the truck might have been converted from a tanker. *(Photo: Peter Davison)*

Gone but not forgotten, Caswell's trucks were always a welcome sight with their smart blue, white and red liveries and scrollwork lettering. The company notched up over 100 years before closing down in the early 1990s, during which time, despite the odd European interloper, it operated a wide selection of British trucks including a good number of ERFs. Much of the company's early traffic involved the movement of steel from the Ebbw Vale works, but Newport docks also provided a lot of work and later diversification into fields such as automotive supply kept this small firm busy. *(Photo: Adrian Cypher)*

Despite favouring Cummins engines, Calor did not purchase CP-spec trucks. Any potential buyer was free to do the same, but ERF made it plain that a non-CP-spec chassis would cost more and have longer delivery time. However, a company with the buying power of Calor probably still cut good deals and were able to plan fleet replacement around delivery times.

This unit joined Calor in 1986 as part of the LPG tanker fleet. This was intense work operating on a two-shift basis between the oil refinery and the bulk storage facility at Port Clarence where a cylinder-filling plant was located. Tractor units usually spent four to five years on the tanker work before being pensioned off to an easier life on cylinder delivery.

When Calor's cylinder business exploded, no pun intended, in 1976/7, due to the Super Ser heater revolution, it found it could not purchase enough new trailers. Consequently many secondhand flats were bought and modified into cylinder carriers like this one. At the peak of the cylinder business the company ran around 1,200 trailers like this. (Photo: Peter Davison)

The standard 14-litre engine offered in the CP range was the NTE320, often referred to as the Super 320. Now reworked, this turbocharged and aftercooled unit was actually more economical than the old E290, but produced significantly greater torque and delivered a genuine 300 bhp when installed in the CP chassis. Raised compression, redesigned combustion chambers and revisions to the injection system were some of the features that combined to make this a fantastic choice for operators wanting good performance from a big under-stressed engine.

For heavy haulage or extreme work, the NTE350 could be specified as an option, but only in 6x4 chassis, where it produced 330 bhp.

With the official designation of CP 38-320, Onward's example makes a fine sight, its slightly muddy condition no doubt the result of farm collections. (Photo: Adrian Cypher)

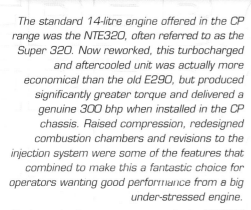

As the Cummins 10-litre engine was considerably smaller in all dimensions compared to the 14-litre, ERF's engineers were able to redesign the engine tunnel with a lower profile to provide more interior space for trucks so equipped. Cabs with the lower engine tunnel were designated Mid-Line whilst those at the original height were correspondingly to be known as High-Line. Factory sleepers retained the distinctive high roof in either case and the second bunk became an option. However, the base for the upper bunk was always provided, but it was now referred to as a storage shelf unless fitted with the mattress. Whilst reworking the various components that made up the engine tunnel, ERF also took the opportunity to improve tooling and construction methods to increase the quality of fit and finish for the rest of the interior, with the dash coming in for special attention. This was all part of the wider CP concept, which saw overall quality improve greatly thanks to the standardised production approach. *(Photo: Steve Lynch)*

ERF had been fitting a Spicer ten-speed gearbox behind its LT10 and Gardner 6LXCT-powered trucks since the middle of 1983 and the two components seemed well suited. However, the CP range was all about economies of scale, which meant using only one gearbox manufacturer, and as its units could be applied across the 11 trucks of the CP range, ERF chose Fuller. Two gearboxes were fitted, the RTX 11609A and the RTX 7609A, though the latter only to the LT10/250-powered models. Both were nine-speed, constant mesh units, chosen for their rugged nature, reliability and serviceability, and for being relatively lightweight. *(Photo: Steve Lynch)*

Despite a decent power advantage of around 25 bhp and 240 lb/ft of torque, the CP38-320 didn't actually out-perform the LTA-290 as much as might be expected. Indeed, on open-road work the two would return very similar journey times, and even on the hillier UK routes, things were fairly evenly matched. However, if an operator's work meant negotiating large conurbations with any regularity then the bigger engine would show its extra power to great effect, allowing the driver to keep pace with cars and stay within traffic-light sequences, thus gaining valuable time in the process. The lower running speed of the 14-litre (1900 rpm rather than the 2100 rpm) and the great wave of torque made the 320 a driver's dream, offering a more relaxed drive with far fewer gear changes required.

For continental work, such as here, which would appear to be regular judging by the European tint applied to the headlights, the CP38-320 was by far the best choice and the model soon became the top seller of the CP range. (Photo: Steve Lynch)

C979 ODP was new to Calor in November 1985 and was used to haul LPG tankers between oil refineries and bulk storage facilities or cylinder-filling plants. Calor standardised on the 6x2 twin-steer layout following the introduction of the 38-tonne limit as its LPG tankers were all two-axle and had very long service lives, 40 years not being uncommon!

Another factor that had a bearing on the 6x2 layout for tractor units was a change to third-party hauliers for the cylinder trailer work, which further lessened Calor's need for 4x2 units.

Given the similarity of the two trucks here, it is reasonable to assume that Jones was the new owner of the Calor truck. Calor's stringent service and maintenance regime would certainly have made the unit a sound purchase. (Photo: Adrian Cypher)

Towards the end of 1985, ERF changed the rear spring arrangement for its 6x2 twin-steer chassis. The new steel/air design replaced the former rubber/air bogie system and gave each axle individual suspension for the first time in three years. The clever design left the Rockwell drive axle suspended in much the same way as it was on the 4x2 chassis with the springs for the second axle mounted lower and overlapping them by just over a foot at their rear fixing.

Staunch ERF users Leicester Heavy Haulage took delivery of two of the earliest examples off the line and, no doubt, monitored the type in service for the factory.

Leicester Heavy Haulage ran a good number of 6x2 C-series trucks, finding them equally capable of STGO operations at up to 75 tonnes, or general haulage work at 38 tonnes. (Photo: David Wakefield)

The Gardner 320 badges proudly displayed here announce the presence of the new 6LYT under these cabs. Launched in 1985, this all-new engine was a 6-cylinder 15.5-litre turbocharged design initially offering 300 and 320 bhp, but with the potential of over 400 bhp if intercooled. The 6LYT was aimed squarely at the Cummins 14-litre unit, and whilst it retained many of the company's traditional values, it was radical for Gardner in a number of features, such as the flywheel-driven helical gear for the fuel pump and auxiliaries. The engine's compact dimensions and the use of aluminium for the crankcase saved weight, making it 350 lb lighter than the Cummins 14-litre.

Lowe put a number of consecutively registered C40s of this spec on the road in 1985. Unusually, the trucks featured a double-drive back end, the operational reasoning for which the author is unaware of, so maybe the extra weight was traded off against the 6LYT.

The Mitchell unit was another of the company's C-series trucks that was uprated for three-plus-two operations with the addition of a Graning axle. (Photos: Steve Lynch and John Henderson)

The CP system, whilst a shock to many of the Gardner fans, was a great success for ERF and undoubtedly saved the company from an ignominious fate in what were very hard times for the industry as a whole. Rationalising parts and building standard trucks reduced overheads at Sandbach by around 10 per cent, most of which was reflected in more competitive pricing for the CP trucks, and it also brought improved quality as the workforce fell into a familiar repeat pattern with each truck that came down the production line. Not only did customers benefit from the price reduction and quality improvements, but also the greatly reduced delivery times that building standard chassis allowed. Indeed, CP-spec trucks were often available from factory stock with immediate delivery and that meant that customer specials, which were still available at a price premium and extended delivery, could be built in as little as ten days, which is maybe why W. J. Daniels reverted from the CP concept for this fine C-series example. *(Photo: Martin Aidney)*

THE E-series
Revolutionary evolution

The E-series was launched in the second week of April 1986 and was to be the final evolution to come from the original B-series design. ERF set aside a £1 million development budget for the project, which, though substantial for a small independent manufacturer like ERF, was a remarkably small figure for such an extensive redevelopment.

This example, which appeared in the initial E-series brochure, was actually a pre-production development model built on a C-series chassis, as is evidenced by the towing loops at either side of the lower grille. ERF had 20 or so pre-production units like this out on the road with trusted operators for evaluation field trials prior to the launch.

Note the subtle launch/demonstrator livery consisting of nothing more than the colour flash behind the door. *(Photo: ERF)*

The April 1986 launch meant the earliest examples were registered on C-plates, making this fine example among the first on the road.

United Tanker Transport was also going through a major redevelopment at this time under the watchful eye of its new MD, Gary Watt. Included in the reforms being put through by the young American were a new blue and yellow livery, stunningly applied here, that was adopted across the 450-strong fleet, and greater control over previously autonomous divisions such as Ancliff and Bulwark. Thankfully for ERF, the buying policy did not change and 31 E10 4x2 units, worth around £500,000, were ordered in August 1986. This example, along with others on pre-Aug 1986 C-registration, must have preceded that order and, therefore, may well have been part of an evaluation batch. (Photo: Marcus Lester)

The most striking difference between the outgoing C/CP-series and the new E-series was the SP4 cab. Whilst still a development of the original SP cab of 1975, and still retaining the SMC panel and steel frame construction method, the SP4 was the most comprehensive update that ERF had made to the design so far. In fact, the majority of the E-series development budget of £1 million went on the cab changes. However, had ERF been tied to a more traditional steel-panelled cab the development costs could easily have been ten times higher and thus prohibitive to such a small company, which proves how prudent ERF had been when it developed the SMC panel and frame system in the first place. Note the protection hoop around the fridge motor of the trailer. (Photo: Steve Lynch)

The E-series range continued with the CP concept introduced in 1984, although the trucks were no longer labelled or referred to as such in the way the C-series versions had been, and the factory concentrated production on chassis constructed from a standard list of components from Cummins, Fuller (Eaton) and Rockwell. Model designation became very simple with trucks built to CP spec being the E14 and E10, powered by Cummins 14-litre and 10-litre engines respectively. Clear badging to this effect was now added to the left of the grille, whilst the ERF lettering was moved from its central position to the right and was now incorporated in a stylised slash, which would also feature throughout the company's marketing. (Photo: Steve Lynch)

Despite the factory's preference for supplying CP-spec chassis, ERF was still happy to build to customer requirements as it always had done, but it made no secret of the fact that delivery and price would be adversely affected in such cases.

Lowe was one customer that ordered a number of early E-series tractor units outside of the CP spec. Broadly similar to the C40 6x4s that the company had previously bought (see page 96) the E-series units were once again powered by the Gardner 6LYT engine, the 15.5-litre capacity of which gave the E16 designation. Unlike the Cummins-engined E14 and E10, which now both utilised an air stack arrangement on the offside, the design of the Gardner engine demanded an air stack location on the nearside of the chassis. It was details like this, which required different parts, and the general economy of scale when buying large numbers of units, such as engines from Cummins, that made non-CP-spec units more costly. *(Photos: Steve Lynch)*

When the E-series range was launched, ERF offered two versions of the SP4 cab; the day cab and the full sleeper. However, an option existed that provided the day cab with a single fold-up bunk and curtains, effectively creating a third type, which was listed as the 'Night Cab'. The provision of a useable bunk within the confines of the day cab was possible because the back panel had been moved rearwards by some 300 mm compared to the SP3 to create a less claustrophobic environment. If the fold-up bunk was not specified, the space provided useful storage.

Outside of the ERF cab options, Jennings also offered a sleeper conversion for the day cab. This involved new panels to extend the depth of the day cab by 230 mm, which brought it close to the 250 mm extra of the factory sleeper. The conversion cost £1,121 and took one week to complete. As with previous Jennings conversions it carried ERF approval and was often used by dealers to meet demand.

This handsome E10 drawbar combination features the day cab and doesn't appear to be fitted with the night cab folding bunk. *(Photo: Adrian Cypher)*

Although the E-series maintained the Cummins/ Fuller/Rockwell CP drivelines, gearboxes for all but the L10-250 powered trucks were actually provided by Fuller's sister company Eaton. The gearbox in question was the now legendary Twin Splitter, which could divide opinion almost as well as it could divide gears, and ERF were the first manufacturer to fit it as standard. Based on the Fuller four-speed main box, and with only four gate positions, the Twin Splitter utilised a unique three-speed splitter to provide 12 speeds. Once moving and with the lever in fourth, further gear selection could be made in a pre-selected manner by moving the three-positioned splitter switch between low, intermediate and high then depressing the clutch when the change was required. With experience drivers could even dispense with the clutch, all of which made for relaxed driving. *(Photo: Steve Lynch)*

Whilst the front of the old SP3 cab had good aerodynamic qualities, courtesy of its smooth, large radius corners and relatively low profile, the rear aspect with its equally large radius corners caused drag by allowing air to flow into the gap between the unit and the trailer. In an effort to improve this, ERF employed the services of the MIRA wind tunnel where it tested 1/4-scale models of the cabs. Not surprisingly, the squared-off design that became the SP4 showed a marked improvement, encouraging the bulk of the airflow past the gap. The square corner also created more interior space and provided a flat edge for the flush fitting of an aerodynamic package, including side extensions, which was developed during the same wind tunnel sessions.

(Photos: Marcus Lester and ERF)

Although it was far less common by 1986, there were still a number of hauliers that found operational benefits in operating the classic eight-legger over extended distances. With this in mind, the type was included from the start in the E-series range and although, as with the tractors, Cummins engines were standard, Rolls-Royce and Gardner were also available. As it was unlikely that the 15.5-litre Gardner 6LYT would have found its way into such a chassis, non-Cummins-powered examples would have been badged as E12, representing the capacity of the Rolls-Royce or Gardner engine. The high headboard would suggest that hay and straw movements kept this example busy, but being badgeless it isn't possible to identify the motive power under the cab. *(Photo: Clive Davis)*

The first 8x4 tipper, an LV cabbed ERF, arrived at Brian Harris, then Harris & Miners, in 1968 and at least one such vehicle was kept on the fleet until closure in 2001. The type, fitted with aluminium drop-side bodywork, was found ideal for handling a mix of loose loads, particularly sand and china clay, and general cargo.

Like the tractor units in the fleet, the eight-legger tippers were true long-distance machines and regularly completed trips to Scotland. Although Riverside Raider, an E10-290, was only equipped with the night cab, its driver, Richard Basson, managed to cope with a week away in its rather restrictive confines. However, a later E10-325 8x4, Widecombe Lad, was fitted with a full sleeper. *(Photo: Marcus Lester)*

ERF were very keen to loose the 'gaffer's truck' tag once and for all with the E-series, so driver comfort was high on the priority list in the design remit of the SP4 cab. To this end a great deal of attention was given to the cab suspension system. Whilst not adopting an elaborate all-independent four-point system like that of the class-leading Volvo F10/12, ERF did develop its most sophisticated system to date with hollow rubber springs and dampers at the front and coil springs and dampers at the back. A great deal of testing was carried out over the infamous paved surface at the MIRA proving ground. The resulting ride was very compliant whilst retaining ERF's trademark poise and feel. In fact, one of the E-series tractor units in the programme recorded the fastest time to cover 1000 miles over that most demanding surface. *(Photo: Marcus Lester)*

The life and times of a truck were often long and interesting. D630 BFA was new to Malcolm Harrison Ltd in 1986 as part of its contract hire fleet. The unit then moved to Bassett and Sons where it was put into their familiar two-tone blue livery. Then it was purchased by Scott Whitehouse, who personalised the livery, without the expense of a full respray, by the addition of the red strip around the cab.

Times were changing in the transport industry when the E-series was launched and although the product was now the best it had ever been, ERF would have to adopt some new thinking in terms of sales if it wanted to stay in the game. One of the biggest changes was a move towards contract hire agreements, which, in the face of changing tax laws that reduced the appeal of buying new vehicles, was fast gaining popularity. The company also introduced contract maintenance through the dealer network in an attempt to entice cost-conscious customers who wanted fixed costs for their operations. *(Photos: Scott Whitehouse)*

Although retaining the high roof principle as introduced on the first B-series factory sleeper, ERF reworked the design considerably for the SP4. The result was a distinctive stepped design, which is illustrated well in this overhead shot of a well-loaded example. Not only did this provide generous headroom above the seats and bunks, but it also gave a small aerodynamic advantage over the SP3 design as it encouraged the airflow over the cab up in two stages. In terms of actual height, the new design was 60 mm higher.

Note the deep ridges that gave the SMC structure strength and, as with the old cab, the provision of an integral illuminated name board. *(Photo: Adrian Cypher)*

The SP4 cab retained the doors, windscreen panel and most of the old front panel of the SP3, including the main grille. However, a marked change was the adoption of single square headlamps in place of the twin circular ones. The new 70/75 Hella units were fitted in answer to the often-criticised dip-beam performance of the old units, but also brought a fresh modern look to the frontal aspect of the cab. The mounting panel and aperture actually went unchanged, the extra space required by the quad system being absorbed by the neat black moulding around the new lamp units.

Bulb replacement was a simple process performed with the grille open to access the rear of the unit. *(Photo: Peter Davison)*

Carl Jarman bought this E10, fitted with the LTA10-290, to replace a Seddon Atkinson 401, which in turn replaced his stolen Gardner-powered C-series (see page 69).

The engine's 275 bhp and 861 lb/ft of torque worked well with the Twin Splitter gearbox and made the truck an economical workhorse. Carl kept the truck for eight years, by which time it was getting on for 15 years old.

Note the firescreened air stack. Knowing that the E-series would find favour with the petroleum sector, ERF paid close attention to making it quick, easy and cheap to adapt for pet-regs. (Photo: Carl Jarman)

The revised interior of the SP4 was a paragon of modernity with all the emphasis placed on making the driver's environment as comfortable as possible. Peter Foden and his team had been highly impressed by the Volvo FL10, which was introduced in 1985, and the influence of the Swedish machine was perhaps greatest in the design of the dashboard for the E-series, which featured gauges and warning lights below a flush, easy-to-clean, flat panel and a distinct angled section that brought the heater controls, park brake and rocker switches within clear sight and easy reach of the driver. All the gauges, and the green band of the rev counter, pointed to nine o'clock when all was well, making a sweeping check quick and easy, to allow the driver's attention to remain focused on the road. The steering wheel, a new soft-touch design, was adjustable for rake and height and positioned to its left was a modern multi-function stork that controlled the indicators, wipers, wash/wipe, headlamp dim/dip/flash and horn. Another modern feature, with which we are now all so familiar, was a three-position rotary switch for the main lights, placed to the lower right of the instrument panel. All cabs, even the day/night version, featured the useful overhead shelf for storage that came with a neat mounting point for a radio/cassette player that was usefully angled towards the driver. Speakers and wiring were fitted as standard, which meant that unsightly holes need not be cut in the interior panels. The materials used in the interior were high quality with fit and finish second to none. The Oregon brown herringbone fabric of the seats, door panels and bunks was both attractive and hard wearing; all gave the E-series the most complete feel of any Sandbach product to date and it very soon found favour with drivers.

The full sleeper version, seen here on the left, came with a single bunk as standard — a second was optional — and a heated version of the Isrinhausen high-back suspension seat.

The night cab, bottom right, is shown with the seats pushed forward and the fold-down bunk deployed, but illustrates the extra room that was gained over the SP3 day cab by the relatively small increase in cab depth combined with the squared-off corners. (Photos: ERF — Author's collection)

Although the E-series chassis followed much the same layout as the C-series, it was now produced in 8 mm rather than 6 mm steel, although the 8x4 chassis had used the heavier gauge on the old range too. At the front, the chassis featured a new drop section, which provided both the bumper mounting and the new twin towing eye positions. Further revisions to engine mounting points allowed all chassis in the range to be the same from the bell housing rearwards, which further rationalised parts, streamlined production and kept costs down. The extra gauge of the chassis brought a small increase in the weight over comparative C-series trucks, but typically only 150—200 kg, not bad considering the revised cabs and better equipment. *(Photo: Dave Kay)*

BOC Transhield placed a massive order for 77 E-series trucks in the autumn of 1987 as part of its fleet-replacement programme. The bulk of the £2.3 million order was for 73 4x2 tractor units like this one, but also included four 6x2 drawbar chassis. The tractor units were fitted with the LTA-250 engine and were downplated to operate at 28 tonnes. The drawbars were plated for the maximum 32.5 tonnes, but were fitted with the LTA10-290 with a view to being uprated should a change in the law allow 40-tonne operation. Apart from the sale, the good news for ERF was that this was BOC Transhield's first purchase of ERF trucks, and its chief engineer, having looked at many competitors, did not consider the E-series a low-spec option, but thought it offered great value through its performance and ongoing operating costs. The trucks were all employed on BOC Transhield's food-distribution contract for Marks & Spencer.

Note the old-style Cummins badge, probably applied by the driver of this unit. (Photo: Steve Lynch)

ERF broke new ground yet again in the autumn of 1987 when it became the first manufacturer to offer Eaton's SAMT (Semi-Automated Transmission). Although automatic transmissions for heavy highway truck applications had been around since the 1970s, they had had only limited appeal for hauliers. Mercedes Benz dramatically reversed that trend with the introduction of its EPS (Electronic Power Shift) at the end of 1985, which proved that modern electronics made such systems a viable alternative to normal manual gearboxes. Based on the excellent Eaton-Fuller Twin Splitter, fitted as standard to E-series trucks with over 250 bhp engines, the SAMT used modern computer control to shift ratios in the box via electro-pneumatic activation of the clutch and gear selectors. A short joystick mounted in a new plastic housing on the engine cover replaced the traditional gear lever. With just a forward and aft movement, the joystick could be used to select gear choice when pulling away, or for skip changes once on the move. An LCD display, mounted in a small pod above the park-brake lever, kept the driver informed of the current gear and suggested when a change up or down was desirable.

ERF initially launched the SAMT option, which cost an extra £2,495, behind the 14-litre Cummins, which, with 330 bhp, produced a truck that was effortless to drive whilst maintaining the economy of its manual equivalent.

Alan Firmin Transport was an early advocate of the system and soon ordered it as standard on its E14 and E10 trucks. (Photo: Steve Lynch)

By moving the indicators down next to the new headlights, it was possible to free up the distinct rounded front corners and equip the SP4 cab with integral air deflectors. Side window and mirror fouling in bad weather had been a problem for all SP cabs since the launch of the B-series. After-market parts, which were widely available, helped, but did not cure the problem. The SP4's integral items were far more substantial and, as illustrated here, did a good job of keeping the build-up of traffic film clear of the mirrors and door glass. Because the deflectors created a high-pressure area, the cab's heater/ventilation intakes were relocated behind them, boosting performance.

(Photo: Steve Lynch)

As the day cab was now longer in its BBC (Bumper to Back of Cab) measurement than the old SP3, ERF had to rethink the cab release mechanism, which used to be at the rear of the day cab and in the seat base of the sleeper. For the SP4, a neat solution saw them mounted in recessed panels behind the doors, which also housed the indicator side repeater. The beauty of this was that all versions could use the same location, which meant fewer parts were required and production was simpler. To tilt the cab, which went to a maximum of 60 degrees, the handles had to be individually released and manually pushed back once the cab was back down; there was no spring loading. The two-piece handle for the cab lift pump was neatly stowed in clips in the passenger footwell. The SP4 tilt mechanism utilised two rams to spread the load and limit distortion.

As a patriotic statement from the UK's last independent truck manufacturer, the cab release handles bore the legend 'Built in Britain'. *(Photo: Adrian Cypher)*

There is no question that the E-series turned around ERF's fortunes, and its timing, which coincided with a buoyant market and exchange rates that did not favour imports, was perfect. By the autumn of 1987, the range had been around for 18 months and with its credibility firmly established ERF swung its attention onto the prestige sector that had previously eluded it and that had been dominated by high-powered machines, particularly those from Sweden, for two decades. With this in mind it launched the 'Supertruck' package, which was aimed at owner-drivers and small fleets looking for a high-profile flagship. The 'Supertruck' package was an option that could be applied to any E14 tractor unit fitted with the NTE-320/350/400 and a full sleeper cab. Outside the spec included the full air-management package, chassis catwalk, coupling lamp, air horn and exterior locker; whilst inside the driver got an air suspension seat, stereo and night heater. Gearboxes were the standard Twin Splitter and SAMT, but the Fuller RTX14609 was also available for trucks fitted with the NTE-400. Engines were fitted with a Jake brake, but were otherwise standard.

For dramatic effect, ERF displayed a 6x4 chassis at the NEC, but 6x2 and 4x2 versions were offered too.

Note the new demonstrator livery with which ERF supplied its test trucks to the press. (Photo: ERF — courtesy of Scott Whitehouse)

Although drivers of the 8x4 chassis benefited from most of the SP4 cab advances, such as more room and better ride, etc., the trim level was reduced to make cleaning easier and prolong service life. To this end, the engine tunnel came with a wipe-clean finish instead of carpet.

The 8x4 chassis was offered in two wheelbases of 5893 and 6477 mm, measured from the centre line of the front wheel to the centre of the bogie, which gave turning circles of 21 and 23.1 metres respectively.

Norde rubber suspension was standard for the rear bogie and diff and cross locks ensured traction across terrain such as this.

Note the standard 60-gallon cylindrical tank, the design of which has not changed in decades, which would not have looked out of place on a truck of the 1950s. (Photo: Clive Davis)

ERF's growing relationship with Cummins reached new heights in the spring of 1988 when it became the launch partner for the new LTAA10.325 engine. This latest development of the LT10 broke new ground for Cummins as it featured an air-to-air intercooling system, with separate radiator mounted ahead of the main one for engine coolant, rather than the air-to-water system it usually employed where a block-mounted heat exchanger did the work of cooling the intake air for the turbocharger. The old method, being all contained within the engine, was good for Cummins as the engine supplier, because it allowed them to guarantee the installation, but with the air-to-air system, a great deal of the installation was the responsibility of the chassis producer. By choosing ERF as its launch partner, Cummins was publicly endorsing Sandbach's engineering ability and build quality.

Although this example was an ERF launch vehicle for the LTAA10.325, it does not feature the '325 intercooled' grille badge fitted to production trucks.

Note the spray-suppression equipment mounted inside the front wheel arches. (Photo: ERF — courtesy of Scott Whitehouse)

The LTAA10.325 put out 304 bhp and 950 lb/ft of torque when installed in the E-series chassis. Cummins had made only minor changes to the basic engine to achieve these figures, most where restricted to the pistons and cylinder heads and gave an increase in the compression ratio to 17/1. New ten-hole injectors and a reprofiled camshaft upped the fuel delivery rate and a new turbocharger from Holset completed the changes. The output of the LTAA10.325 was almost identical to that of the Volvo F10 with the TD102F (intercooled) engine, a truck generally considered as one of the class leaders at the time, but gave significantly better fuel economy, giving ERF a serious contender in the 38-tonne tractor sector. (Photo: Marcus Lester)

Silkolene ran an all-ERF fleet for the own-account delivery of its oil products. Whilst articulated tankers handled bulk loads of a single-grade product, rigids like this were used in place of compartmentalised tankers to handle mixed grades. The system used square aluminium tanks mounted on pallets, 12 of which could be carried in the curtainside body.

The company was heavily involved in the early days of truck racing and the Silkolene C-series, piloted with great vigour by Willie Green, was a crowd pleaser in the mid to late 1980s. Originally fielding a full-spec sleeper, Willie soon changed to a more nimble day cab. The truck enjoyed a degree of factory support during its campaigns. On one occasion, following a big smash at Swedish Grand Prix, the badly damaged cab was totally rebuilt by ERF's Middlewich facility in under two days so that Willie could make the next round at Donnington the following weekend. (Photo: Steve Lynch)

Van Hee Transport, Tyneside's finest, was operating around 40 trucks by the early 1990s and the family-run concern had largely standardised on Scanias for its mixed rigid and artic fleet with 6x2 113 tractors being favoured for 38-tonne operation. However, during the previous decades the company had enjoyed a great deal of success with the Ford Transcontinental and it was the similar driveline offered in the E14 that attracted its first ERF purchase. As it was ERF's standard offering for a 6x2 layout, and therefore the most economically priced, the D-registered truck was a twin-steer, when Van Hee's first choice would have been a tag axle, but the truck soon proved itself with the 320 bhp Cummins returning an average of around 8 mpg with curtainside and flat trailers. Three more E14s followed on E-registrations and a further three on F-registrations. Although the company was no longer sending trucks to the Middle East, a regular destination for its Transcons, the E14s were despatched to the continent with no qualms. *(Photos: Adrian Cypher and Steve Lynch)*

The E8 was a significant addition to the range introduced in the autumn of 1988 and powered by the Cummins 8.3-litre straight-six engine with air-to-air charge cooling. The basic turbocharged version of this engine had been available in the USA for two years and Europe for about one, but ERF was the first manufacturer to offer a new intercooled version, the 6CTAA-265.

The engine weighed just 565 kg, about 300 kg less than the LT10, and gave 245 bhp and 704 lb/ft of torque when installed in the E8. About 600 lb/ft of torque was available for most of the rev range over 1000 rpm, which, combined with an excellent all-synchomesh 9-speed gearbox from Eaton, made performance surprisingly good.

The E8 was commendably light, weighing well under six tons even with a full sleeper cab and ready to go, which made profitable 22-tonne loads a real prospect, with careful trailer choice.

As well as the new engine and chassis changes, the E8 also featured the first reworking of the SP4 cab. Designated the SP4A, this would be fitted across the range.

The E8 had a basic price of £34,000 and with its high earning potential was an ideal choice for work up to 32.5 tonnes, a sector that still accounted for nearly 50 per cent of the heavy trucks in the UK.

Plumb Center found the E8, down-plated to 28 tonnes, perfect for its own-account work. This example was a pre-production model, hence the E-registration, and the first E8 operated by the company. (Photo: Steve Lynch)

When Ketton Cement, Tunnel Cement, Ribblesdale Cement and Clyde Cement amalgamated in 1986 to form Castle Cement, the result was a massive 400-strong fleet and the UK's second biggest supplier of cement. The corporate livery of red and white was adopted at the same time and was first applied to six E12 8x4 tankers formerly of the Ribblesdale fleet, which numbered 97 ERFs at the time.

Although its own-account work involved moving some three million tonnes a year, Castle Cement found a drop-off in demand in the early 1990s gave it spare capacity which it filled with bulk powder movements for third parties. (Photo: Alan Watts)

As the LTAA10-325 required components outside those of the engine manufacturer; namely the radiator and associated plumbing for the intercooling process, it was the responsibility of ERF to design, develop and source them within the exacting parameters set out by Cummins.

The result was neat and compact in its design, and the trunking, which ran across the top of the engine, fitted easily under the SP4A cab without the need of modifications to the floor. Although the intercooler fitted in front of the truck's main coolant radiator, its depth was not so great as to require any changes to the front panel and the design was such that the header tank for the main radiator could stay in its original position.

Note the extra ERF grille badge and the trailer's lift axles for empty running. *(Photo: Peter Davison)*

There haven't been many fleets as well respected as Gibb's of Fraserburgh. Perfect envoys for the industry, Gibb's finally called it a day in May 2002 as dwindling fish quotas and crises such as BSE hit its core business.

The family firm reached its optimum size of around 25 trucks in the 1980s and maintained that level to the end. Drivers were allocated to a truck and generally stayed with it until replacement, spending up to five days a week away and clocking around 80,000 miles a year on work that could often be multi-drop throughout southern England. ERF always featured in the fleet, though DAF and Seddon Atkinson, both using the Cabtec cab, were much in evidence towards the end.

Refrigerated trailers were built to Gibb's' spec by neighbouring Gray & Adams and always featured Carrier units, which were preferred for their exceptional reliability. (Photo: Steve Lynch)

The most significant, and noticeable, change that came with the SP4A cab revamp was the new combined bumper and airdam arrangement, which followed the modern trend started by MAN with its F90 in 1987 and which marked out the Cabtec cabs for DAF, Seddon Atkinson and Pegaso, which appeared shortly afterwards. The neat design incorporated steps in the front aperture, which also served as the tow pin locations, depressions ready to take optional fog lights and even a raised section for mounting the number plate.

This handsome example, fleet name Gentle Giant, was one of a pair that were bought new by R. T. Keedwell. The driver, Fergy Howe, had around 40 years' experience with the Somerset haulier at the time of writing in 2014 and was then driving a Renault Magnum in the blue and cream livery. (Photo: Clive Davis)

Steve Tabner was given this vehicle on his first day at Tankfreight. The truck was brand new and allocated to a dedicated contract with British Edible oils, originally sporting their logo on the doors. It operated with this smart two-compartment trailer delivering throughout the UK from Van Den Berghs' Bromborough depot. Tankfreight flourished on contracts such as this, a similar one, worth around £75,000 a year, employed another E10 artic combination to deliver liquid Propane and Butane for Handygas, whilst a three-year deal with the MOD to supply aviation fuel to two RAF bases in the South-West was worth £250,000.

Tankfreight put over 100 trucks on the road with these YUA registrations, mostly ERFs and Volvos. Steve would later change to F101 YUA, another E10, but with blue livery, that effectively did the same job, but not under fixed contract.

The truck is seen fresh from the cleaning, a process made simpler by the facilities that the company established throughout the UK and which it operated under the name Tankclean. *(Photo: Steve Tabner)*

This fine cattle-carrying example, with its glorious fresh livery, shows to good effect the new three-step layout that was part of the SP4A cab revisions. Often criticised, work on this area had been ongoing since the original B-series and had been improved with every cab development along the way. Although clearly the best yet, the new three-step design still met with disapproval from some drivers, who found the step spacing too close. However, a great improvement to cab access was made by revisions to the A-pillars and door hinges that made near 90-degree door openings possible for the first time on any SP cab. (Photo: Alan Watts)

Over the years, huge resources have been dedicated to the development of the car transporter as designers and engineers constantly strive to find clever ways of accommodating more vehicles per unit. Although this Hoynor trailer represents one of the less complex approaches, it could still handle eight family cars by virtue of its tilting decks. The type was also popular due to its sturdy design and the quality of its manufacture.

Although the day/night cab gave a significant improvement in interior headroom over the C/CP-series, it still offered a low profile, measuring under 3 metres tall to the top of the roof and only 3150 mm to the top of the air stack, which made it ideal for this sort of work. *(Photo: Clive Davis)*

This most interesting vehicle was unusual, even in Calor's varied fleet. Built in 1989 and based on an E10 with a short rigid chassis, it was commissioned for the transport of bulk storage tanks from Calor's refurbish facility in Stoney Stanton, Leicestershire to Calor depots nationwide from where the tanks could be delivered on to the customer by smaller trucks equipped with a crane. The trailer was built on smaller wheels to allow tanks to be carried one above the other in the special framework and the Cummins 250-powered combination operated around the 26-tonne mark. The trailer was later altered to carry just a single height of tanks and the truck was fitted with a crane to enable it to make direct deliveries to customers. These often tended to be in rural areas, which were beyond the mains supply. On these occasions the trailer could be left at a convenient location whilst the truck made delivery, returning to collect it later.

Note the different chassis paint in the later photo. Calor adopted this darker grey in 1990, but also applied the new colour to refurbished vehicles after that date. The wide adoption of aluminium wheels to save weight also saw the end of red-painted wheels on Calor trucks at this time.

(Photos: Iain Carr)

The Eagle has landed! Putting the emphasis back on the Eagle name was a welcome return for many enthusiasts and a shrewd marketing decision by Perkins, which took over the Rolls-Royce engine business in 1984. Although the Eagle name had never gone away, as such, the later developments of the famed 12-litre engines from Shrewsbury had been heavily marketed with the 'Li' designation bestowed on them. The Eagle TX was essentially a new engine, but it retained the same bore and stroke as the old design and was in fact a side development of the 800-series developed by Perkins in collaboration with Leyland. Leyland had exclusive use of the 800-series but Perkins was free to develop other versions for the market.

ERF had never stopped listing the Rolls/Perkins engines, but since the CP-series they had fallen outside of the preferred spec and become a cost option. However, ERF were quick to announce that it would fit the TX range and actively promoted the option, probably as it had an eye to sales in northern Europe where Leyland was enjoying good sales of Eagle-powered T45s. *(Photo: Clive Davis)*

ERF first showed a chassis fitted with the new NTE-365 at the NEC show in October 1988, well ahead of the Cummins' launch, which was planned for early the following year. The 6x2 chassis featured the '365' power output in the name board of the sleeper cab, but was otherwise devoid of badges relating to the engine other than the standard E14 fitted to the grille. The NTE-365 was part of the engine manufacturers Phase-2.5 development for big 14-litre units, which would result in them being redesignated 'Super E'. Various changes were made under the Phase-2.5 programme in the pursuit of higher outputs and cleaner emissions. These included a new intercooling/charge-cooling system that Cummins named OAC (Optimised After-Cooling). This was simpler than previous systems and more efficient over a greater range of temperatures without loss of performance. Other changes to the camshaft, compression ratio and turbocharger resulted in useful increases in output. The Super E-365 produced 340 bhp installed in the E-series chassis and effectively replaced the old E14-350 in the range.

Note the extra horizontal cooling slots that were provided in the bumper/airdam assembly for trucks powered by the new Cummins engine. *(Photo: Adrian Cypher)*

Although devoid of an operator's name, this E14 could well have been part of Jack Light's largely anonymous fleet, it was certainly employed on the concrete pipe movement that was the Holcombe haulier's speciality and many of his trucks were painted in this shade of green. Although Jack tended to favour European trucks, he would consider any high-powered tractor at the right price and was no stranger to the E320 Cummins, already having operated a Seddon Atkinson 401 that was so equipped. Jack would, no doubt, have been impressed by the Super E365, as shown by ERF in October 1988 before its official launch, but even better news was to come for those with the need for a truly high-powered tractor unit when Cummins announced the Super E465 in the following March. Listed as the NTAA-465, this engine, like the LTAA-325, now featured air-to-air charge cooling. (Photo: Clive Davis)

The design of the front panel on the SP4A cab was much cleaner than its predecessor and no longer required the split and cutouts in the grille to give clearance for the hinges when tilting the cab, which resulted in this much neater appearance. The entire front panel, grille included, raised on two gas struts to give excellent access to daily check items, but the struts proved weak in service and would often fail. The front panel also featured reshaped corner deflectors with pronounced upswept vanes. The location of the indicators in the bumper/airdam assembly made them vulnerable to damage, but the entire corner of the bumper was now easily replaced and designed to be semi-sacrificial. *(Photo: Alan Watts)*

This Nexus E10 displays the new corporate TDG livery as introduced in 1990. The TDG did not initiate an immediate rebrand to its entire fleet as it had so many autonomous companies under its umbrella that it would be uneconomic to do so, especially in the midst of a recession. The first TDG company to adopt it was Beck and Pollitzer. In each case the company name was given greater space, but the Juggler logo was prominent in all cases. The logo was supposed to represent the ability to manage many tasks whilst being witty and charming! Note the specialised steel carrier trailer with its central bay for steel coils like the one being lowered in and its neat sliding frame cover. (Photo: Alan Watts)

ERF announced a minor update to the SP4A cab late in 1990. However, the changes that made it the SP4B were mostly restricted to the interior so it was not possible to distinguish it from the outside.

The main change was to the instrumentation, which now featured an integrated circuit board and dials that all pointed to the 12 o'clock position when all was well. There was also a new centre storage unit on the engine tunnel and a change in

seat and bunk fabric, though the overall colour scheme was much as before.

Anglo Hargreaves ran a number of E10s, including 8x4 tippers, in power stations such as Rugeley, where the trucks performed the essential jobs of moving coal in and ash out. It is doubtful that the truck and trailer combination in this publicity shot would have stayed so pristine once working in this dirty environment. (Photo: Alan Watts)

Helmsman, as the name suggests, can claim routes firmly established in 18th-century Bristol in the glorious days of sail when Britannia really did rule the waves and required great quantities of ships' tackle to keep the situation that way. The company evolved in parallel to the shipping world, switching to boiler production when steamers ousted sail in the 1800s from its new premises in the London Docklands.

The modern company moved to its present location in Bury St Edmunds in 1970 and now specialises in the production of lockers of the type used in schools and industry.

The company used to operate an own-account fleet, which consisted of 4 ERFs, but a decision to use an outside haulier brought this to a close in 2008. J475 TFL was one of the last two units operated by Helmsman.

Note the after-market roof spoiler, complete with Helmsman logo, and the revised exhaust, which appeared late in 1990. *(Photo: Peter Davison)*

The Eagle TX range went from strength to strength following its initial introduction, finding favour with hauliers who required more torque than produced by the Cummins LT variants, which spanned the same bhp range as the first TX engines.

By the time that the E-series was in its final years of production, 1991—93, ERF listed four versions of the Eagle TX, spanning 300—400 bhp.

When this E12 was new, the Sweeting Empire consisted of ten family businesses that had evolved over many generations from just one. Between them the companies ran 80 trucks. This bizarre situation, which saw each branch competing for the same work, was not only distinctly English, but also quite possibly unique. However, the livery was broadly similar across the different companies and the attention to detail second to none.

Note the sun visor fitted to this superb example, an option not often fitted to later E-series trucks. (Photo: Clive Davis)

The relationship between Richard Read and ERF was a long and enduring one that stretched back to the 1950s and was born out of good old-fashioned values and trust. When suddenly faced with two new vehicles that he could not pay for due to a customer going bankrupt, Richard Read approached the factory, only to be told to pay for them when he could. This he duly did, but no interest was added and ERF's only request was that he bought more of their trucks. Richard went one better and actively promoted sales, which led to commission payments and eventually to him becoming the appointed distributor for Gloucestershire and Herefordshire.

The spec of Read's own fleet was always a good measure for outside observers: from this unit you could tell that the company considered that an E14 producing 320 bhp was more than adequate for 38-tonne operation.

Note how the exhaust silencer also provided a step on to the battery cover for chassis access. (Photo: Adrian Cypher)

The E-series was developed from the original B-series of 1975 and was replaced in the summer of 1993 by the new EC-series, by which time it was effectively an 18-year-old design, albeit one that had been regularly updated over the years and was still very competitive. As ERF was a component assembler, the E-series also benefited from the constant improvements to the driveline made by the various suppliers as their products were developed for the market in general. Despite the obvious improvements of the new EC trucks, particularly the cab, many hauliers lamented the passing of what had become something of an old friend. The last examples, registered on L-plates as seen here, were highly sought after and would become popular on the secondhand market in due course. The sound engineering, rust-free cab and generally high build quality of the E-series endowed the trucks with very long potential service lives, as is illustrated here by this log-hauling 8x4, which was still grafting in one of the toughest sectors in 2014.

Note the hole for the airstack in the roof fairing of the tractor unit. This was a very late revision only affecting the last E-series trucks and was contrary to ERF's original stance that the airstack would function normally with the air-kit in place. *(Photos: Marcus Lester and Clive Davis)*

BERESFORD
A gentleman haulier

Although it could trace its history right back to the turn of the 20th century, when John Beresford started a small haulage business in Tunstall, Beresford Transport as known, loved and now sadly lamented by enthusiasts really started when his son, Ken Beresford (Snr), set up his business in 1953. Being based in Tunstall, the northernmost town of the five that made up Stoke-on-Trent, meant that there was plenty of potential work for his new venture,

Beresford were quick to paint the ex-Earls Court Show truck, JRE 389N, when it arrived at Tunstall in the glaring orange paint scheme that ERF had applied to the three chassis that it had exhibited. This is the second, updated, livery, which the company applied after a few years. (Photo: Ken Beresford Collection)

courtesy of the numerous potteries in the area. Indeed, it was an early contract with the tile giant H. & R. Johnson that would prove highly significant to Beresford Transport for the next 40 years.

Ken Beresford (Jnr), having studied at the Royal College of Art in London on a four-year scholarship as an art, design and music teacher, joined his father's business following his national service. His first posting for Beresford Transport was a baptism of fire at the company's Liverpool depot where Ken learned all he needed to know about man management and running a haulage operation. He returned to Tunstall and took over the running of the entire business in 1967. Ken was very much cut from the same cloth as his father, a highly respected man, and his approach, based on the highest levels of professionalism with the utmost attention to detail, saw the business grow steadily and expand into continental services. The smart appearance of the trucks and its wide field of operations made the fleet one of the most recognised both at home and

P-registered B-series trucks started to appear in numbers at Beresford Transport. This impressive line-up of rigid six-wheelers are painted in the Cristal livery representing the tile products of H. & R. Johnson. This was one of Beresford's most important customers and accounted for the movement of around 900 tons a day in and out of H. & R. Johnson's facilities. (Photo: Ken Beresford Collection)

abroad. Ken's keen business acumen also saw the company purchase strategic sites such as the old BRS yard in Tunstall and land in Longport, the latter providing a much-needed parking facility for around 90 of the company's 150 or so trailers. The purchase of the old BRS depot provided space for the growing fleet and came with 40,000 sq ft of warehousing that allowed Beresford to offer storage to key customers, such as H. & R. Johnson, and room to assemble groupage loads for onward delivery.

Beresford's relationship with ERF, which was just nine miles down the road in Sandbach, started when the marque was established in the 1930s. Ken's grandfather started buying ERFs for his company, by then known as Beresford, Caddy and Pemberton, which made Beresford one of ERF's oldest customers and it remained a loyal one right up to the time of its closure in 1994.

By the time of the B-series launch, Beresford had nearly 40 years' experience of operating ERF trucks and had established a clear preference for Gardner engines, so it was, perhaps, inevitable that Beresford would take delivery of one of the original B-series show trucks from the Earls Court launch in 1974; that it would be the 8LXB-powered unit was a given. As a pre-production chassis, it led a slightly charmed life, benefiting from constant attention from the factory at Sandbach with modifications and improvements made as and when required. However, it was very much a working truck and Beresford found it performed very well and particularly liked the cab, which was a marked improvement on the A-series trucks it was running. More and more were added to the fleet in the following years and by the end of the decade the company operated 60 examples.

Ken's approach to running a fleet meant that trucks were always purchased outright. This way they became company assets, which could be parked up in

ERF's inability to supply the B-series with a sleeper for several years after the launch allowed Seddon Atkinson through the door at Tunstall. Ken knew Peter Foden very well and his views were taken very seriously at Sandbach. Ken's purchase of Seddon Atkinson 400s and his persuasive argument for a sleeper version of the B-series was instrumental in its creation.
(Photo: Ken Beresford Collection)

quieter times if necessary without the financial consequences of hire purchase or a contract hire agreement. Vehicle life was approached with a similar view. A nominal period of six years was allowed for depreciation, but whilst a truck remained presentable and profitable it would be kept on much longer — eight - to ten years for a B-series would not be uncommon thanks to the sound engineering and rust-free cabs.

C-series units were purchased following their introduction and from 1983 the company favoured 6x2 units to accommodate the 38-tonne limit. The last ERF type purchased before closure was the E-series.

Ken Beresford stood proudly with one of his latest ERF E-series units in the late 1980s.

Ken's position in the local community led to the unusual request to deliver this telephone box to France. The box was a gift to mark the twinning of Congleton Borough, which included Sandbach, with Trappes, a town 15 miles from Paris. Not only was the iconic structure delivered, for a nominal fee, but it also arrived on the back of a truck produced in Sandbach operated by one of the UK's most recognised fleets on the continent. (Photo: Ken Beresford Collection)